Some Words for
Just Do What Works

JUST DO WHAT WORKS pleasantly surprised me as I admired the author's grit and determination to do what was best for her students, rather than the traditional opinions expressed of what a teacher should do. While reading, I kept thinking that Katherine Boerner is the teacher I wish I had when I was a child in a classroom. Her ability to connect with students who had experienced difficulty in class reminded me of the anonymous quote about teachers: Students don't care how much you know until they know how much you care.

Katherine definitely cared about her students, and her students knew it, and that is why she was capable of lighting the spark that created a passion for learning in students. In addition to being a masterful teacher, Katherine is also a gifted writer. Throughout this book, Katherine doesn't just tell, but she shows how to ignite success in the classroom. I was unable to put the book aside as I became so involved with the students she brought to life in the pages of her book, and my vast admiration of her immense teaching skills which encircled her care and concern for her students grew.

If you are a parent, read this book. If you are a teacher, read this book. If you are a student who wants to become a teacher, read this book. None of you will regret it.

—*Jean Sasson*

International bestselling author of
13 books about the Middle East, including
Princess: A True Story of Life Behind the Veil in Saudi Arabia

With Love and Commitment...

Just Do What Works!

LESSONS OF TRUTH,
RESILIENCE, AND VICTORY
FROM UNEXPECTED SOURCES

Katherine A. Boerner

Write Way Publishing Company, LLC

Printed in the United States of America
ISBN 978-1-946425-07-2
Library of Congress Control Number 2017910371

Book design by CSinclaire Write-Design

Book cover by KlevurAuthor photograph ©2017 Laura Kesler Photograph LLC

Write Way
Publishing Company
Print . Digital . Audio
Write Way Publishing
Company LLC

Just Do What Works!

DEDICATION

To my *life-focusing* gifts from heaven,

Clarkson and Kylene

Table of Contents

Foreword

TEACHERS ARE NATION builders—a universal truth of all modern societies. In our society, we value teachers who place a premium on listening to their students and who try to take them forward from where they are rather than trying to shoehorn students into a preconceived mold.

This belief in the fundamental role of teachers as nation builders is the main reason I *loved* reading Kathy's book. Her stories will tug at your heart strings as she shares lessons she learned along her own educational and personal journey into the world of teaching. These stories give insight and hope to not only teachers but all adults about the importance and struggle of finding one's way in structures that do not always reward innovation.

Kathy started teaching in the most challenging of ways when she began mid-school year. At that time, she did not meet the departing teacher and was not even allowed to see the classroom in which she was to teach—you will learn why in one of her early stories. At twenty-one, fresh out of college and feeling ready to teach, it would have been almost impossible for Kathy to anticipate the challenges of her very first teaching assignment.

Another reason to love this book is the rare privilege of reading so many great stories about real kids and the successes they achieved simply because of the commitment of a caring and dedicated teacher. I had the pleasure of having Kathy share many of these stories with me over the years and am thrilled she took my advice to write them down. Because she made a point of staying in touch, Kathy helped me crystallize a belief of mine—that once my student, always my student.

You may, in reading these stories, react somewhat like I did. Some will make you laugh. Others will make you cry, maybe even make you angry. But you also will delight in what happens with Kathy and with her students as she grows into a confident teacher and adult—after shedding many of her own tears as she learned to "just do what works."

Enjoy, celebrate, and support our valuable teachers, who are essential in reaching the vast and endless capabilities of our youth. These stories definitely show that schools need to attract and retain more *Kathys* in teaching!

— Charles R. Coble, EdD
Professor Emeritus, Science Education (1972-1996)
Dean, School of Education,
East Carolina University (1983-1996)

This Book Is About

THIS BOOK IS about kids being people. It is about morals and ethics. It is about doing what is right, regardless. It is about using compassion and thoughtfulness in getting to know people, helping people, being friends with people, regardless of age, color, creed, or background. It is about learning to let go. It is about time and patience. It is about humor. It is about faith. It is about a young woman who feels she has the weight of the world on her shoulders because she knows her work affects children's lives and the direction they take. It is about her knowing she is less than prepared for the challenges ahead of her, and how she fights outward and inward barriers to ultimately find what she needs is to ...

"just do what works."

Why Puzzle Pieces?

PEOPLE ARE JUST like pieces to a puzzle ... their purpose is destined to perfectly fit together and ultimately help complete a beautiful picture we call life. Along their journey in seeking their place in life, people are privileged to meet others who are also searching for their place in their picture-perfect puzzle. Sometimes paths only cross for a short period of time with the privilege to help, guide, and lift each other up along the way.

The people in this book belong to different puzzles yet for a brief but precious period of time, we gathered inside my dilapidated, old trailer that we called our classroom and made our own temporary but wonderful picture-perfect puzzle.

— *Kathy Boerner*

Introduction

I HATED SCHOOL! Absolutely nothing about it appealed to me, so it is amazing that I not only became a teacher but loved the profession!

Though I received a solid formal education, it wasn't until I learned to "just do what works" that I became more successful working with my students and later even with my own children.

Just do what works does not support "the end justifies the means" mentality. We need to adhere to morals and laws while we help, guide, and encourage others. What it implies is that *our* opinions of *how things should be* don't matter. What truly matters is that we successfully reach the hearts of others, which allows us to ultimately help them.

I shared many of my classroom stories with Dr. Coble, a former professor of mine, and he encouraged me to write them down. I don't think either one of us ever thought the stories would end up as a book, but I am thrilled they have.

The names and even a few genders have been changed with all the children mentioned in this book. Most of the names have been changed with the adults, but I did keep a few of the real names since they are true heroes, and I want to make sure their stories are heard. Those names are Dr. Coble, Miss Watkins, and Mrs. Martin.

Though the stories revolve around a classroom, the lessons and thought-provoking situations within the stories can be helpful to all adults: teachers, parents, supervisors, managers, business professionals—-anyone who deals with other people.

As you read the stories, I know you will fall in love with all the children. It is my wish that you will also keep your mind and heart open to the valuable lessons these children have to teach us.

Never Say Never

IT WAS INSANE! I was sixteen and in the eleventh grade, and yet I was being guided (more like pushed) by the school system to make academic decisions that would start determining the direction of my future. This unsolicited push was due to the fact that SAT testing was fast approaching. In my circle of friends, everyone seemed to know what they wanted to study in college and the degrees they wanted to pursue. As for me, all I knew was what I didn't want to be. Without question, I was positive that I would *never* be a nurse or a teacher. Period! End of discussion. I'm not sure why I didn't want to become a nurse, but there was no question to why I didn't want to be a teacher. Simply, I hated school!

Though I *played the game* of school and college well, there was really nothing I liked about either one. To outsiders, I'm sure I seemed happy. I always got along with everyone, rarely ever missed school or classes, and earned good grades, but I was basically just going through the motions. At such a young age, I didn't realize that I was miserable because I was trying to survive in a world where my personality and learning style weren't even thought about, let alone considered important. I was just part of the masses and simply needed to do what I was told. It was as if I were on a massive treadmill going nowhere and learning very little of substance. The teachers and professors were different over time, but the routine was the same year after year. I struggled playing this game, and behind my smile, I always thought there was something wrong with me.

My well-disguised despair wasn't because I didn't want to learn. On the contrary, I loved learning, but most of what I had to study and was required to do in school and college seemed pointless. I felt, for the most part, that I was given information, expected to commit it to memory, and then required to regurgitate it back to the teachers and professors in ways that fit their personalities and belief systems. My absolute distaste for the education system was sealed by the quizzes and tests. The indirect or direct use of these measuring techniques to manipulate and control students seemed endless. The results of these devises were used to define how my classmates and I measured up. In a way, it was as if the tests defined our worth and value.

The structure of college was more appealing to me, yet the immature students and the egocentric professors did tend to be more challenging and exhausting as I continued to play the game. Part of the game in college was being required to declare a major very early in my studies. This seemed almost impossible since I had numerous interests but no burning desire in any one area. Oddly enough, after changing my mind several times, I was able to decide on a major due to my swimming background.

I was on the university's swim team and also was a lifeguard, which meant I was Red Cross certified to teach swimming lessons. During the second semester of my sophomore year, I had a free two-hour block of time between my classes. I heard that the university offered swimming instructions to local elementary students, so I volunteered to be one of the instructors. The time I had available to teach just happened to coincide with a special education class. Though

I definitely wanted to help children learn to swim, I was extremely nervous and unsure how to handle special needs children. My fears quickly melted away as I realized that I enjoyed the role of a teacher. Then, and over the years, I was delighted to see that my personality created a unique connection with any student at any age. Shortly after volunteering as a swimming instructor, I declared my major in special education. Amazingly, that meant that I was going to become a teacher! *Never say never.*

Dr. Charles Coble

IT ONLY TAKES one excellent teacher or professor to change an attitude and ultimately the life of a student. I should know because it happened to me. I was privileged to have Dr. Charles Coble as the professor for one of my classes in college. Though I only had him for one course, he made an incredible impact on my college experience and my life.

During the first semester of my junior year, I was required to take a science course for education majors that Dr. Coble taught. While every class of his was packed with interesting information, I also saw that Dr. Coble was positive, energetic, and enthusiastic about everything he taught and everything he did. Because of his teaching style, students rarely were absent since no one wanted to miss what he had to teach. If that wasn't impressive enough, Dr. Coble was always willing to talk with any of his students, current or past. Remarkably, even with his very demanding schedule, he was never too busy for any of us.

One extraordinary technique that separated Dr. Coble from so many other professors was that he actively checked on his students outside of class. I believe he did this to see how the students were progressing with their assignments and their working knowledge of the information he was teaching.

He wasn't interested in just doling out facts and expecting students to absorb the material; he wanted to make sure they understood the information and learned how to apply it. If Dr. Coble saw any of his students around campus, rest assured he would end up talking with them, asking questions about class and the work they were doing. Students never seemed to mind talking with him and most welcomed his conversations.

During this required science course, Dr. Coble assigned several long-term projects. One in particular I didn't see any purpose for but I still wanted to do a good job with it. I was required to gather some of the information from the science section of the library. When I did my classwork there, I always sat in the back of the enormous room. At that time in my life, I was very reserved and didn't care to mingle with people I didn't know.

One day, when I was researching information in the library for this assignment, Dr. Coble came to visit his students to see how we were doing on our projects. I thoroughly enjoyed listening to Dr. Coble in class, but I was petrified to talk with him one-on-one, so I always managed to create escape routes in order to avoid talking with him directly. That particular day, I watched him closely and planned to leave before he got to my table as I had done many other times, but I miscalculated his next move. He skipped over several tables and came directly to mine. Now I was stuck and had to talk with him!

I don't even remember what we talked about at first because I was so nervous. Slowly I calmed down and began to enjoy our conversation. Though I played the part of a happy student, Dr. Coble skillfully picked up on my negative feelings and became determined to help change my attitude. He would stay five to fifteen minutes with most students in the library, talking and discussing whatever needed to be dealt with, but he spent much longer with me. After almost an hour of genuine interest in me, Dr. Coble succeeded in energizing me not only about my assignment but also about school.

Through Dr. Coble's probing questions, he discovered I was interested in photography. Instantly, he decided to adjust my assignment in order to incorporate my photography skills. A part of the assignment was to sketch a branch of a tree, noting its changes over time. Dr. Coble told me to use photography to track those changes instead of sketching them. We chose a special dogwood near campus and for the next year, far longer than the class lasted, I developed a complete documentation of that tree from three different viewpoints. I even put the photographs to music! After hundreds of slides and endless hours, the project was complete. For several semesters, this completed project was highlighted and shown in Dr. Coble's science education classes as an example of modifying assignments to help a student. It was also shown over several years during the annual Statesville Dogwood Festival in North Carolina.

Dr. Coble took me, a student who was just going through the motions at school, redirected my thinking, and helped me see great possibilities that were ahead for me. He sparked my interest using a skill I was developing on my own and tailored an assignment for me because I was more important than the lesson plan. By doing this, he also proved to me that the information I was learning was important and not just something done for a grade. As a student and then a teacher, I realized that confident teachers, when necessary, were able to pull themselves away from their lesson plan and adjust their methods to reach the students and still cover all the required material.

I was blessed with wonderful parents who always told me how smart and talented I was and that I could do anything I wanted. It wasn't until an outsider, an educator, validated what my parents kept telling me that I started to believe I had special talents and needed to use them. Then, through observing Dr. Coble, I learned what was necessary to become a successful teacher. In addition to thorough knowledge of the information to be taught, the obvious characteristics of an effective teacher (or parent) include commitment, positive energy, honesty, consistency, and enthusiasm. Additionally, there are other crucial elements most adults miss in their efforts to reach a child. They definitely need to be an open-minded, willing, and confident person to *listen* to the needs of the child because each child has wants, desires, and dreams just as adults do.

Children are not empty vessels for adults to mold into what they want. Children are not their parents, grandparents, or others to whom they are compared. Children are unique and come to us full of personalities and talents just waiting to be unveiled and released. In tandem, as we help children find their hidden treasures, they also yearn to be loved, accepted, and understood. Whether they are our students or our children, we adults need to stand by our children and with love and commitment "just do what works" to help them become the precious people they were meant to become.

What an Honor

DESPITE MY FEELINGS toward college, I took my studies and grades very seriously. With that said, I always completed my assignments and received good grades, but I never felt that I was important–only the grade was important. Since I believed just the grades were important, I learned how to play the game by feeding professors what I knew they wanted to hear. Though it was exceptionally frustrating, I learned not to let playing the game bother me too much since my true dream was to be a wife and a mom. I wanted to be a stay-at-home mom to raise my children, and I believed that my education degree would allow me to work outside of the home, if need be, while my children were in school. It seemed like a great plan, but there was one flaw. My senior year was nearing and there was no fabulous candidate in sight for a husband, so I knew I would have to get a job teaching.

After graduation, I was secretly hoping the interviewing process would take some time since I still thought Mr. Perfect was going to magically appear and sweep me off my feet. Well, neither happened: Mr. Perfect didn't arrive and the interviewing process didn't take long. I went on two interviews the week after I graduated and was offered both jobs on the spot! Sadly, I didn't want either one. Where was Mr. Perfect?

I can see in retrospect that I needed the career in teaching and the time to mature to prepare me for what I wanted and now have: a great husband and two wonderful children. Through the numerous years of teaching, I received valuable lessons from my students both by working with them and for them. It didn't matter whether I was teaching in a regular classroom or a special education classroom; every situation had endless lessons waiting for me to learn. When I began teaching, I struggled to meet the needs of my students, but as I conquered those demands, I grew in confidence, courage, strength, and commitment. I developed skills and discovered talents I never knew I had that allowed me to become the person I am today. For that, I am grateful to the wonderful students I taught.

Over the many years I was a teacher, I had an incredible opportunity not only to help students develop their academic skills but also to be a positive influence in their lives. When I was a resource teacher working with students who had academic and emotional challenges, I understood that my classroom was the last chance for many of them to receive personalized academic and emotional help within the education system. They may have been young, but I knew the clock was ticking as they were losing their aspirations and interest in school. Frustration and discouragement whittle away at anyone's desire to accomplish something, and this is especially true with children. Without some kind of positive influence, I believed failure would consume their natural desire to learn, and many children would choose to give up on school, or worse, give up on themselves. This realization brought incredible responsibilities and pressure, but, over time, I grew to learn that being a teacher was a privilege and an honor.

Miss Watkins

BEFORE I WENT solo with my own classroom, I had to be under the tutelage of a certified teacher as I fulfilled my student teaching requirement in college. I requested to be placed near my hometown so I could live with my parents and save some money. Little did I know that in an effort to be financially frugal, I would be given the privilege to work with an incredibly talented and skillful educator. Throughout life, we encounter people who come into our lives and stay; we also encounter many who come and go. With some of the people who come and go, we have negative experiences, but then there are special people who come and go, and yet in their short time, they have a profound and positive influence in our lives. Though she was only in my life for a few months, Miss Thelma Watkins taught me inspiring lessons as a teacher and as a person. One important lesson she taught me is the inspiration for the title of this book.

I was assigned to complete my student teaching under Miss Watkins' guidance. She was the special education teacher at a large elementary school. I never knew for sure but I think Miss Watkins was in her mid-thirties. She was a tall, strong-looking woman with the smile and demeanor of a sweet and gentle person. Every day when she came to work, she was professionally dressed and held herself to a high standard of performance. That was in direct contrast to the younger teachers who dressed and behaved very casually. While Miss Watkins may not have influenced dress or behavior codes for other teachers as much as she did with me, everyone who knew Miss Watkins held genuine respect for her. Over my few months working with her, I was fortunate to have a front-row seat that allowed me to observe her successfully reach and teach many students who were not expected to be able to learn much, if anything at all.

My days of student teaching are a faint memory, except for my first day. Miss Watkins greeted me warmly and invited me to sit at a round table suited for first graders with seats to match. We chatted for a while about surface topics but Miss Watkins gradually changed the conversation to the task at hand, which was to get me involved with the students and to tell me what she expected of me over the semester. She revealed that she was aware I had been as she said "an excellent student at the university," but in the same breath, she claimed that none of my achievements at the university guaranteed success in the classroom as a teacher. Elaborating, she explained that her job was to teach me strategies and give me experiences that I would not have been exposed to in college that were nonetheless essential to reach my students successfully. She believed there was one strategy that I needed to learn immediately. With that said, Miss Watkins leaned over the small table toward me, lowered her voice almost to a whisper (I believe to make sure I was listening), and shared her main strategy for being a successful teacher. With confidence in her voice, she told me "to forget everything I learned in school and ... *just do what works!*"

What in the world did she mean by "forget everything"? Here I had suffered through almost four years of higher education, playing the game, jumping through senseless hoops, and now I was being told to forget it all! On the surface, that was the way it sounded, but what I learned was that I did need my background in education, although I would also have to think on my feet and develop my own solutions using bits and pieces of everything I had learned. I couldn't rely on any particular theory or method someone else had developed and then proceed to struggle making it work for all my students. Miss Watkins accurately pointed out that no student or situation would ever fit perfectly into any theory or method I had studied. Life and people weren't that predictable and neat. So many times throughout my teaching years, I learned that I would have to create a one-time-only solution for a child because that was what was necessary. All I had to do was to be creative and observe how the student responded and learned the best.

Miss Watkins successfully applied her approach to special education students, but I learned that her method, or rather philosophy, worked with anyone at any age. Her strategy was the foundation for the way I taught throughout my teaching years and was the reason for many of the successes my students achieved. I also believe it is the reason I have been a successful parent.

This approach required me to work around the students' needs instead of the students working around mine. It meant that my classroom wasn't mine, and the methods used were not for my benefit or ease. Instead, the classroom and methods were to offer my students a place and experiences that allowed them to feel comfortable and confident. Building this critical foundation knocked down barriers that were holding the students back and allowed them to learn more readily no matter what they needed to learn.

I can't recall specific situations in Miss Watkins' classroom, but the creative and positive attitudes I gleaned from this incredible person are permanently etched in my heart. I do remember, though her days were rarely smooth and often had many trials, Miss Watkins was always energized and hopeful for what the next day would bring. I had the privilege to witness day after day the loving and committed efforts of a humble yet determined teacher as she wrapped herself around the needs of each of her students. They all loved her and worked hard for her. Because of Miss Watkins' dedication to her students, their lives and mine were changed forever!

First Impressions

I MENTIONED EARLIER that I went on two interviews and was offered a position by each school. At the conclusion of each interview, I asked to see the classroom where I would be teaching if I accepted the job. Basically, I just wanted to meet the children and get a feel for each room. Oddly, the principal of the school where I ended up working deflected my request by claiming that he was not allowing any of the applicants to view the class so as not to disturb the students. With my trusting personality, I accepted the principal's excuse, and I naively judged my potential teaching situation from this school's outward appearance. I was also excited that the school was in a good area for apartments. Based on those factors, I accepted the job as a resource teacher at that school. All I knew at that time was that I was going to be giving supportive instruction to kindergarten through sixth grade students who had mild educational and emotional challenges. I never once suspected there was a deceptive reason the principal kept the room a secret.

The main school building was clean, orderly, and attractive, but off to one side of the building, at the edge of the playground, was an old, beaten up, single-wide trailer. That was my classroom! The trailer itself was a concern, but what was happening inside was the real problem.

My first day in the classroom was my first day on the job. I should have known there was a serious problem inside when the principal walked me to the door of that small, single-wide trailer and left without introducing me to the students. Walking in, I quickly surveyed my room and the students. It was frightfully obvious that the room basically was used as a holding facility rather than a classroom since the atmosphere, condition of the room, and the behavior of the students were dead giveaways.

As for the room, the walls were bare, showing off grimy, putrid green paint with only a crooked clock nailed up. There were papers, pencils, and books scattered on the floor, the desks, and the shelves. Two of the twelve small windows had cracks that were mended together with household masking tape that was in the process of peeling off. The indoor/outdoor rug was filthy and probably the main cause of the stench in the room. There was a make-shift wall of bookshelves about five and a half feet tall which divided the small interior in half. This allowed another class to meet on the other side, but it also made my classroom quite tiny.

Perusing the room, the handful of educational supplies on display gave the false appearance of academics being taught. A closer look revealed that the supplies were still neat and clean, which exposed the sad truth that they had rarely, if ever, been used. Throughout the day, I realized that worksheets and workbooks were the main educational tool used and that whatever work had been completed was usually not even graded. I quickly learned that the students were allowed to eat candy and chew gum during class, despite the fact that both were against school policy. Plus, I was enlightened by a few of the older students that every Friday was game day. It was painfully obvious that the principal didn't hold the resource teacher to the same standards he did for the rest of the school faculty. It appeared the resource teacher's only responsibility was to keep her students out of sight and quiet.

Though I was not expecting such a wretched condition for a classroom, I knew I could fix that. What I wasn't expecting, or prepared for, were the sad and angry faces that greeted me that fateful day. It was obvious the students didn't like losing their previous teacher midyear, but what I couldn't understand at first was why they were so hostile to me. It didn't take me long to figure it out. It was the color of my skin. God gave me pale skin. I had nothing to do with that, but I must admit, over the first few months of teaching, I did wish I had at least a tan to ease some of the tension.

It didn't take long for the Caucasian students to decide they didn't like me either. I guess they didn't like the fact that I ended the candy-eating and gum-chewing freedoms and immediately dropped game day. None of these decisions were very popular with any of the students. So, between the principal and the students, I had an uphill battle ahead of me because I had different plans in mind for this classroom other than it just being a depository for children. I never could have imagined the amount of work and emotional stress I would have to endure to reach my goal.

I know for the first two years I cried almost every night or at least I'm sure that's what it probably seemed like to my parents. I was living with them during this time until I could afford to move out. Thankfully, the lack of money helped me yet again because I was so fortunate to have my parents' complete moral support and great advice daily, which helped me keep things in perspective as I waded through the quagmire in my classroom.

Even with all the assistance my parents gave me, the pressure and demands were quite taxing. To begin with, I was never prepared to handle the heart-wrenching pleas I received from some of my students' parents. Many of these parents would explain that their son or daughter didn't qualify for any other type of assistance. That meant my class was their last hope for any extra help! The parents confided in me about all their struggles dealing with their child's educational, emotional, and medical issues and looked to me for answers. Other parents divulged personal information blaming themselves for their child's problems, as if God was punishing them through their child. It broke my heart to witness the guilt and anguish these parents lived with watching their child suffer. I did have a few really obnoxious and downright nasty parents and an equal number of almost perfect parents. The majority of the parents I worked with, though they may not have known how to accomplish it, truly did want to do the right thing for their child.

The majority of my students were from poor families. A few students were from rather wealthy families, and some were from middle-class families. Whatever economic level or educational level these parents came from, it was obvious that in their way, most of them loved their children. It just seemed that many of them didn't really know how to parent. Loving a child and parenting a child are two very different actions. Many parents were just children themselves in age or in maturity. Their business meetings, love lives, shopping sprees, or manicures were just some of the many and pitiful excuses they gave me for not being able to assist their child at home.

Unfortunately, some of the problems my students faced at home were not just the absence of good parenting skills; sometimes it was the absence of parents. After school, many of my students would go home to an empty house. It wasn't just my older students either; it also happened with my very young students. They would be alone for hours after school, fending for themselves. Many would have to feed themselves, if there was even food in the house. Then, with some rare cases, a few of my students' real problems would start when the parents came home; these were the nightmare parents.

The combination of the parents' pleas and their personal issues, the serious academic and emotional needs of each student, and my inexperience left me feeling extremely overwhelmed. Many nights I would cry from pure exhaustion from teaching and worrying about my students' personal lives. Most mornings, I would cry all the way to work because I felt so inadequate to deal with the serious challenges each day brought. To survive, the only thing I could do was to take one day at a time and use a lot of Kleenex.

I learned quickly that the typical approaches I had learned in college were not going to help me overcome my challenges and help me reach my students, so I dove right into using Miss Watkins' method of *just do what works*. I constantly tried to think of ways to work with each student and find new and creative methods that might help them learn concepts and how to apply them. My efforts rapidly consumed my life. My friends teased me because all I would ever talk about was "my kids" and the situations I would have with them. Despite all their teasing, my friends became very interested and concerned about my students' developments and grew to ask for updates. It was hard, even for outsiders, not to get emotionally involved with my precious students!

Initially, I believed that none of the teachers or anyone in the administration cared about my students or me. Because of this incorrect assumption, I felt quite alone and vulnerable. As I worked more and more with the other teachers and staff members, I learned that there were awesome and supportive people in the school who willingly worked with my students and me. Fortunately, it was only the first principal and a small number of teachers who really didn't care about my classroom or me. That one principal and the few teachers made it very clear that as long as my kids and I stayed quiet and out of sight, they would be happy. That definitely wasn't going to happen!

The old adage "Don't judge a book by its cover" was so true in regard to my rationale choosing a school. The clean and professional look of the facility gave off the air of success and support throughout the school. Little did I know that inside the book's cover, in this case, walls, was a hidden secret tucked away in a rickety, old trailer that was my classroom. My first impression may have been wrong about the school and where I would teach, but in the end, the life-changing events that took place inside that room truly made a wonderful, lasting impression.

Difficult Teaching Conditions

THIS IS AN important chapter as it reveals the outrageous teaching situation I was assigned, so please take a deep breath and bear with me as I describe the convoluted intricacies of my job.

My official job title was NCR teacher. That acronym stood for non-categorical resource teacher. The non-categorical label was definitely accurate. The students who qualified to be in my classroom, via a large battery of tests, were students who were identified as educationally challenged, learning disabled, emotionally handicapped, and gifted and talented. A student could have one or a combination of each challenge with the exception of gifted and talented. Students identified only as being gifted and talented attended another class.

During the first three and a half years that I taught at this school, my students ranged from kindergarten through sixth grade. Then, over the last two years, my students ranged from kindergarten to fifth grade when the school district moved the sixth graders to another school.

A distinct characteristic of my students, with the exception of one, was that they looked like other "normal" students in school. Their differences only showed up when they tried to perform academic tasks or were put in stressful situations. I taught twenty-seven to thirty-five students each year and as long as a student was at the school, he or she stayed in my program year after year. That meant I was able to work with most of my students for years. I had the privilege to work with a handful of them for the full five and a half years I was at the school. Because of the opportunity to work with my students continually, many of them felt like my own children and, in some cases, I became part of their real families.

Every day, each of my students had to report to his or her regular classroom and was responsible for much of the work in that class. Students came to my classroom for whatever subject, subjects, or issues where they had documented difficulties. Initially, many of the classroom teachers expected any student in their class who also came to me to do all the work in their classroom, even if it was in a subject that was well above the student's ability. Rightfully so, my students felt that coming to my class was a punishment since they had double the workload. It took a while but, eventually, I was able to work things out with most of the classroom teachers and alleviate the duplicated workload.

Scheduling students to come to my room was twofold. First of all, I was supposed to have students come two, three, or five days a week. On paper, it seemed like a sensible solution. In reality, skipping days caused confusion for the students, the classroom teachers, and me. Having struggled the first few months with this scattered schedule, I began rewriting each student's Individual Education Program (more commonly referred to as I.E.P.) to officially schedule each of them to work with me daily. This change was graciously accepted by both the classroom teachers and the parents. The regular classroom teachers never minded the extra days my students were out of their classes since their rooms were always at or over capacity, and the parents were thrilled that their child would receive more personal attention.

The second part to scheduling my students was accommodating the period of time they were required to stay in my room. Children could be in my room from thirty minutes to three hours. The thirty-minute slot was a joke since there was no way anything of substance could be accomplished in just a thirty-minute slot, no matter how minor an issue a student had. On the other side of the spectrum, three hours wasn't always enough because some of my students had multiple and serious issues that demanded much more time. It was easy to correct the thirty-minute restriction because all I did was rewrite the I.E.P.s upgrading the time to an hour. The only way I could solve the latter problem though was to unofficially, but with the parents' permission, work with those students far longer than the three-hour limit.

Technically, I was supposed to schedule students to come see me during the time their regular classroom was studying the subject where they were having difficulties. Simple? Not a chance. Teachers never taught the same subject at the same time, so I might have five students on the same level, but they were from different classes and needed to come five different times. If I was unable to have the student come during the optimal subject period, I would ask the teacher when the next best time would be for the student to come. The universal answer was "recess." If there was ever a child who needed recess, it would be a student with a learning or emotional challenge. It took so much more energy to stay still and stay on task when the work expected to be done was challenging that my students needed time to let go of all their pent-up energy and just enjoy—so recess was never my choice.

An odd challenge I had with my students was to schedule them so they all could fit in my room. The first three and a half years, I shared my small, single-wide trailer with another class. Having just half of a small trailer, I could only fit so many bodies in there at one time. I was able to schedule and fit more of my older students at one time since they didn't do too much moving around, but my younger students, though smaller, were much more active and took up more space.

In addition to scheduling my students to come to my room, I also needed to schedule time to work with students who were assigned to me on a consultation basis. Those students didn't come to me. Instead, I was to work with and monitor the student in his or her regular classroom, assisting the teacher and student in any way I could. I can't say I ever found a solution to my scheduling dilemma, but many wonderful teachers helped me by being graciously flexible.

My next obstacle was all the paperwork. Oh, all the repetitious forms. I'd like to meet the person who supposedly read all the papers that were sent to Central Office. We had forms for observations of students, forms for referrals to the Student Based Committee, forms for referral for psychological testing, forms for referral to Academic Placement Committee, forms to show placement in a certain special education class, forms for showing what was to be accomplished for the student while in class, forms for retesting, forms for parent approval, forms for exiting a program, and forms for transfer to a new class or a new status. Forms, forms, and more forms.

Most of the information had to be repeated on every form. Each form had four copies and had to be handwritten, so I was always getting cramped fingers from pressing so hard to get through to the fourth copy. Each copy was color-coded: white went to Central Office, yellow went to the school, pink went to the teacher, and the green copy went to the parent or some mysterious place when the parent wasn't involved. It was nearly impossible to keep up with all the changes to a student's file since there was a folder for each student at Central Office, with the regular classroom teacher, and with my program. Too many people were involved with the students' folders, so the folders rarely matched. I understood the need for paperwork to track the events taking place with a student, but a great deal could have been done to streamline all the repetition and to increase accuracy across the folders.

If the scheduling and paperwork didn't frustrate me, the meetings I had to attend sure made a last-ditch effort. I hated meetings. I thought they should be brief, to the point, and infrequent. The meetings I had to attend seemed long, fruitless, and far too frequent. I would do my best to miss as many as I could, but that was never a popular decision with the administration. I had so much to do to prepare for my students each day, I began to resent all the time I felt I wasted filling out the endless forms and going to unnecessary meetings.

Scheduling, paperwork, and meetings continued to haunt me throughout my teaching years. I felt then, and still feel now, that teachers are asked to do far too much outside the classroom, diluting their efforts in the classroom. Needless paperwork and meetings were and are some of the biggest offenders in taking away time from teaching work. For me, I avoided both paperwork and meetings as much as I could.

In order to survive the daily challenges of my erratic schedule and to meet the variety of needs my students had, I desperately needed to prioritize where my time was best spent. Though I tried to do it all at first, I quickly learned it wasn't humanly possible so I had to choose what was important. Hopefully, the stories that follow will reveal what I chose and that I chose well.

Three Girls

I KNEW IF I was going to be successful in my classroom, I had to establish my rules in the class quickly and at the same time win over the children. Neither was going to be easy since the students were used to very lenient rules, and many of the students seemed to be racially biased. I had a handful of troublemakers, but three girls in particular were the catalysts to many of my problems. At the young age of ten and in the third grade, these three girls were the main instigators for many of the disruptions in my classroom. When they were together, trouble was just moments away.

Toni was the ringleader of the three and a royal pain. She was average in height and size for a ten-year old. She had a beautiful face and had deep brown eyes. Her smile was usually devious but on off moments, I would get a glimpse of her genuinely radiant smile. Toni always came to school well-dressed from top to bottom, and she always wore intricately corn-rowed hair. Unfortunately, her behavior and attitude were not so attractive. Toni was curt, rough with her mannerisms, rude, obnoxious, and downright nasty. Can you tell I didn't like her very much?

The other two girls were Mya and Morgan. Mya was

simply gorgeous. She was tall, thin, had stunning jade eyes, a smooth complexion, and a smile that was incredibly charming. She was very sweet and mannerly plus quite gregarious when Toni wasn't overshadowing her. Morgan was petite and also very pretty. She was somewhat withdrawn so her personality didn't stand out as much as Mya's, but Morgan was kind, sweet, and funny, again when Toni wasn't around. Both young ladies were clearly nice girls when they were not under Toni's influence.

Unfortunately, the occasions without Toni were few and far between, which meant disruptions in class were inevitable. Many times when Toni would act out in class, her classmates would start to laugh. Their laughter just fueled her creativity for more conniving acts. Toni may have only been ten years old but by creating bedlam, she had more control over my class than I did. I had no clear plan for what I should do to get control, but I knew I had to do something—and it had to be fast!

Because I started midyear, I decided to keep each student's schedule the way their previous teacher had it so I could maintain normalcy for the classroom teachers and the students. The schedule definitely was not optimal for me, but it was doable. Doable that is, except for the schedule with Toni, Mya, and Morgan. The girls were in the same classroom and their teacher wanted them to leave at the same time so as not to disrupt her classroom too many times, and I certainly understood her position. That meant I was going to have to figure out how to control the girls when they were in my classroom.

One of the milder occasions, but one that seemed to make a lasting impression, took place during a reading session I had with just the three of them. At first, they were semi-civil, but it didn't last long. I had asked Toni to read but she refused. She instantly leaned over and whispered to Mya and Morgan and seconds later, the three of them slid from their chairs onto the floor and under the reading table. For just a moment I sat alone above the table listening to the giggles from underneath. Having grown tired of all their games, I was not about to let them get the best of me or destroy my class again, at least not that day!

I took my books, along with the girls' books, and crawled under the table with them! Their defiant laughter subsided when they witnessed this crazy teacher not yell, scold, threaten, or chastise them but instead, crawl under the table and position her dress neatly (I always wore a dress, stockings, and heels when I taught). I placed the books in front of each girl and continued right where I had been so rudely interrupted. I asked Toni to read the same page I had asked her to read before when we were above the table. She refused again and just stared at me in disbelief. Staring right back at all three, I simply told them that no matter where they went, I was going to be right beside them making them do their work. I may have sounded stern, but I had to fight to keep from smiling as I looked at them uncomfortably scrunched under the table with heads bent and astonished looks on their faces. By the looks on their faces, I knew I had gotten their attention.

According to their I.E.P.s (Individual Educational Programs), each girl was (supposedly) able to function on a second-grade reading level. I had specifically chosen mid-first grade work for them to ensure that they were successful. Plus, I wanted to build up their confidence and create a positive interaction with them. I politely asked Toni to read, but she stiffly refused yet again. As my voice became harsher, she got even more defiant. Then she snapped at me saying that she already knew how to read and she didn't need to read "no baby book" as her head moved side to side like a metronome.

Finally, the light came on in my head. I realized that this child couldn't even read a first grade book and here I was going to humiliate her in front of her followers. I truly didn't want to belittle her, but I knew I had to show who the real leader of this class was, so I confronted her. Using a soft voice this time, I let her know I was aware that reading was hard for her and that I knew her horrible behavior was just to cover up this truth: she couldn't read. Of course, she refuted my accusations at first. Then huge tears welled up in her eyes, and she became silent. My heart melted when I saw her struggling. I decided to take the attention off of her and put it on the other girls. Speaking to Mya and Morgan, but indirectly including Toni, I told them that they were all reading in what they called baby books and if that was what they wanted, fine, but not while they were in my room. They were going to put up with me and learn how to read harder books whether they liked it or not. I reminded them that everyone in my class, including me, needed help with something. I also pointed out that it was best for them to learn in my room rather than in their regular classroom of twenty-five students who would more than likely tease them. In my room, I promised them there would be no teasing and laughing at anyone for the work they were doing (and there never was).

Staying under the table, I changed gears again. I used the same books, which they had refused to read earlier, and quickly tailored the lesson to see how many a, b, and c letters they could find on a certain page. I had the girls write each of the words they found in columns building their own personal reading word list. As they searched for words, I morphed it into more of a game, and we ended that class having our first positive experience together.

This was one of my first important lessons (and I had numerous ones) on flexibility and thinking on my feet or rather, in this case, sitting down! Over the next few weeks, I was amazed to see how quickly the girls' behavior began to improve, and my overall classroom became more productive. These beautiful girls not only needed someone to care about them, they needed someone to be truthful with them and hold them to a higher standard. More importantly, over time, they learned that they could succeed if they just put in the work!

I could never have imagined that the four of us would end up building such a wonderful bond from the way our relationships began. These girls were so special to me. I grew to love and admire their spirit and their unique personalities. Though I still had a few bumps to work out with all three of them (more with Toni), I was grateful I had three and a half precious years with them.

Toni

THE THREE GIRLS may have improved as a whole, but Toni was still trying to get *one up* on me, and I struggled not to let her. It seemed as if I was always on the defense. Though I knew in sports that games could be won because of a good defense, I never thought it would ultimately be a good tactic in a classroom.

During one class, Toni was acting out again so I reprimanded her for it. Her snarky reply threatened that she was going to tell her mama on me and her mama was going to whoop me good for scolding her. Without hesitation, I called her bluff. I countered that I was delighted with her idea because I had been trying to contact her mother but couldn't reach her. I added that whatever it took to get her mother to the school was fine with me because I had plenty to tell her about what her daughter was doing. Needless to say, I never heard from her mother.

Sadly, when I did need to meet with Toni's mother to have updated paperwork signed, she refused to cooperate. With every call, the mother grumbled saying that she was too busy and I was wasting her time. On one occasion, she even yelled at me over the phone for bothering her and claimed that it was up to the school to set Toni straight! Since I had to get her signature to approve Toni's continuation in my program, I literally had to leave school over my lunch period, go to her place of work, sit myself down in front of her and say "we have to talk"! I did manage to get her signature, but it wasn't a pretty scene. This woman's attitude and manners were worse than Toni's! No wonder Toni struggled with her behavior.

I believe the breaking point between Toni and me was when she, once again, refused to read. At the reading table, she stood up as if to leave. I knew the work wasn't too hard for her this time, so I was going to make her sit back down. I was fed up with her attitude. As soon as she stood up, I was over beside her. I quickly put my hand on her shoulder with a firm grip. She looked at me, at my hand and back at me with the most disgusted look. Then she said, "Get your white hand off me!" Without even thinking, my reply was simply, "As soon as you get your black fanny on that seat!" With that, I proceeded to quickly press her back down in her seat. I know Toni was shocked with my response—and so was I! As soon as Toni was in her seat, I immediately changed my disposition and resumed class with a smile as if nothing had happened.

Fortunately for me, news traveled fast and from that time forward, we never had a black/white problem again with any of my students. The best part about this story is that from that point on, Toni and I started getting along very well and even began enjoying each other's company.

I definitely learned that some battles, even in a classroom, could be won by a good defense!

Mya

AS I MENTIONED, Mya and Morgan were quite manageable without Toni around. I never had any trouble with Morgan, other than the fact that she was a follower and got in trouble due to her association with students who were troublemakers. As for Mya, she and I got along very well when Toni wasn't around except for one situation.

My students may have been making many improvements with their behavior and academics but I always seemed to have to deal with their old habits of procrastination and follow-through with their work. My lone altercation with Mya was because of her procrastination with a particular in-class assignment. It was review work that shouldn't have taken very long to complete, and I knew she was quite capable of completing it. Her old habit of thinking she couldn't do the work popped up, and she just plain refused to do it. Mya tried to argue with me, but I was not going to give in to her pleas and she knew it. She just got more and more frustrated. While she was arguing with me, she was standing in the middle of the foyer's archway, holding a book. I am sure her frustration just got the best of her and the only response she had to my continued request was to hurl the book that she had in her hand in my direction. The book flew right at me and, thankfully, I had good reflexes and caught it. Instinctively and with no ill intention, I tossed the book right back to her! I didn't throw it hard, but it did hit her and then fell to the floor. When the book landed, I barked, "At least you could have caught mine! Now go do your work!" and I walked away.

Before the end of class, Mya handed in her completed work. I quickly checked it so she could see how she had done and was thrilled when she saw she earned an eighty-seven. She was also pleased to see that most of her errors were due to minor mistakes, so she really did know the material. I gave her a big hug, told her I knew she could do it and that I was so proud of her.

The bell rang as I was finishing my conversation with Mya and in a whinny voice, she begged not to do any more of this type of work. To her disappointment, I told her she would have similar work to do but as for the next day, she and I were going to be doing something different. I motioned for her to bend down so I could whisper in her ear. As soon as she heard what we were going to do, she got a huge grin on her face and giggled out loud, "Oooowwha, Miss Chann-da-ler!"

The next day, we played catch!

Walls

IT DIDN'T TAKE me long to see that the placement and condition of my classroom was of little interest to the administration and more specifically, the principal. I heard many excuses as to why I was expected to tolerate the horrible condition of my room: "It is just temporary" or "The budget is tight this year" were the constant excuses, but I believed the real reason was that I worked with *those students*. Granted, the first year and a half, the other side of the trailer was used for the gifted and talented class but after that, his class was moved into the building while my class stayed in the trailer to share with the speech and audiology teacher (who only used her side of the trailer for a few hours a day, a few days a week while I was there all day every day! Others may have fallen for the principal's politically correct excuses he habitually gave me, but I sure didn't. It was obvious by his lack of attention and concern that he just wanted to keep my kids *and me* quiet as he hid us off in whatever shabby trailer was available because my kids didn't matter.

As for the gifted and talented class, I thought it was a waste of time, money, and talent. I also felt that the classroom space could have been used more effectively by me, but it was obvious that the needs and wants of the gifted and talented class came first because the *smart kids* needed to be guided and nurtured. Please don't misunderstand me. The children in that class were *wonderful* and needed to be challenged. The teacher was the problem. I was told many times by that teacher how smart he was and how well he did in college. He even went as far as to brag about how much he made, which was a heap load more than I did!

Sadly, none of his academic successes or high salary guaranteed that he would be an effective teacher. Usually in his class, he handed out worksheet after worksheet, or he would show history films. There were rarely any class discussions or student interactions with any of his activities. He normally would sit at his desk, drink coffee, and check the worksheets as they were completed. For a well-touted, gifted and talented teacher, he had absolutely no drive or creativity. I may have been the lowly non-categorical resource teacher, but I know the children in the gifted and talented class would have learned more valuable lessons with thinking and exploring their talents on my side of the bookshelves!

One example of the many outrageous things I had to cope with by having to share with the teacher of the gifted and talented program was when he would show his history films. Of course, he would need to turn off the light and that meant *all* the lights in the entire trailer went off because there was only one switch. Some days I would literally have to teach the whole day in the dark! My complaints to this teacher and the principal seemed to land on deaf ears because they both seemed to embrace the same attitude toward my class; the classroom conditions were just fine because—I just worked with *those students*.

If the situation with the other teacher wasn't bad enough, I also had to deal with the condition of the trailer itself. The inside walls were hideous. In addition to being a putrid green color, they were stained and dirty looking. The walls were so ugly and depressing I had to do something, so I asked the principal for permission to have the walls painted. I must have lost my mind to think I could get some help from the principal or at least that is what he may have thought because I actually got a snicker as he snorted out an abrupt "No."

Not willing to take a "no" for an answer, I asked if I could buy the paint and paint the walls myself. I even offered to paint the whole trailer inside so the students in the gifted and talented class would have a better environment too. I was certain that he wouldn't turn down that generous offer. How wrong I was! The snicker was replaced with an annoyed "No!" Quite perturbed with me and using a condescending tone, the principal explained that he could not allow me to paint my room because it would make the other teachers look bad! I am not sure what *the other teachers* had to do with me painting my hideous trailer walls, but it did show me that the principal was all about orchestrating the impressions of others he thought mattered so he looked good. After hearing the rest of his feeble excuses, I was fuming inside but on the outside, I kept my cool. I had decided not to make any waves since I had just thought of another solution to my problem.

The principal specifically told me that I wasn't allowed to *paint* the walls. He did not tell me that I couldn't cover them with something else. Over the next several weeks, I collected rug samples. This was during the time when rug samples were free for the asking. I went around to every retail rug company I could find and asked for whatever samples the businesses were willing to give me. After I had collected a huge number of samples, I went to my trailer over a weekend, and I nailed up all my rug samples covering the hideous walls on my side of the trailer. When the samples were all up, my room looked absolutely adorable! I couldn't wait for Monday to come because I knew my students would be so thrilled with their new "rugged" walls.

Regarding the principal, I didn't think I could lose. I would either get scolded or I would get scolded and have to take down the rug samples. If I had to take down the samples, big holes would be left in the walls since I used large nails to secure the rugs. It would be a health hazard to have holes in the interior walls, so the repairmen from the Department of Education would have to come, fill the holes and then paint at least my side of the trailer. I felt I would win either way.

The funny but exasperating part of the whole story was that the principal never came into my room the rest of that year to see what I had done. See how important my class was? Nevertheless, my students loved their new walls and they would boast to their other classmates about the *cool* classroom they had. We never got to solve the problem with the lights being turned off but a side benefit of having the walls covered with the rug samples was that it deadened the noise from the films being shown, so we weren't bothered as much while we worked in the dark.

Initially, my ugly wall situation may have been frustrating, but it turned out to be quite useful. Over the next five years, my colorful and free rug samples were used over and over as I moved each year to a *new* rickety, old trailer.

Classroom in Demand

DURING THE FIRST few months teaching, it was obvious by the whispers and the judgmental looks that some of the staff and faculty, along with most of the students, believed my classroom, the resource room, was for dummies. Because of this, I knew I needed to work very hard to change that impression. Creating a new reputation is one thing but changing a bad reputation to a good one is exceptionally hard. Unfortunately, this bad reputation was quite apparent to my older students so just getting them to my class was not always easy.

One student in particular, who was extremely embarrassed to come to my class, was a fourth grader named Thad. Thad may have been the shortest student in his grade but he was good looking and very athletic. He walked and talked with great confidence, wore a Polo shirt almost every day that was starched and ironed to perfection. His golden blonde hair was down to his earlobes and was immaculately cut and never out of place. Thad was so revered that most of the guys wanted to hang around him and many of the girls wanted to be his girlfriend.

Because of his popularity and the reputation of the resource room, it almost killed Thad to be part of my program. In order to get to my class, he would try to sneak out of his regular classroom, hoping that his departure wouldn't be noticed. There was little chance of that since the girls noticed his every move. I had other older students who, at first, were not thrilled about coming to class, but they eventually got over whatever issues they had. Thad, though, had serious self-image issues, and it was heartbreaking to hear the lies he would tell his followers as to why he had to come to my class.

Despite the fact that Thad didn't want to come to my class, once he was in the class, he and I worked very well together. Reading was a bit difficult for him, but math was exceptionally hard. Over a short period of time, Thad experienced consistent successes that caused him to feel more confident about his work but sadly, he still hated to leave his regular class to come to my class. After a few months working together though, I was delighted to receive an indirect compliment from Thad showing me that his attitude toward my class was becoming a bit more positive.

It all started with Thad and his girlfriend. His girlfriend wasn't just any girl. Jennifer happened to be the star student in the gifted and talented class! Of all the girls to pick! I must admit Thad did have good taste because not only was she smart, she was really sweet, funny, and as pretty as Thad was handsome. The problem with Thad and Jennifer was that she attended the gifted and talented class that was held on the other side of the bookshelves!

One day I heard Jennifer ask Thad why he was attending my class, which everyone in the school referred to as *the resource room*. I knew I needed to help him out since I'd heard him struggle on other occasions, so I interrupted their conversation. I confessed that I heard Jennifer's question and said that I was excited to explain to her what my class was all about. I told her that the resource room was mostly for students having trouble learning a subject and asked her what subject gave her troubles. She thought for a moment and then replied, "Advanced Geometry!" Without cracking a smile, I pointed out that everyone needs help in one area or another. Then I apologized, explaining that my class was full during the day but I added that if she'd like to come to my room after school, I would be happy to help her with her geometry. I only met with Jennifer a few times but she learned that Thad's class was hard as well as helpful. Objective accomplished!

Thad's actual indirect compliment came when I overheard another conversation he was having with one of his buddies in the cafeteria. His friend was interested in the resource room and wanted to know more about it. Thad willingly explained the process to be approved for my class. Then, with an excited voice, he talked about what we did in class and gave some examples. The friend seemed quite enthusiastic about what he had heard from Thad and inquired how he could get into the program. After a very short pause, Thad just looked at him in a very confident manner and said that he was sorry that the class was full, but maybe Miss Chandler could work with him after school!

Priceless Internal Pride

ONE OF THE many personal battles I admittedly never won as a teacher was keeping my room organized. It wasn't that I didn't try but with twenty-seven to thirty-five students coming in and out of my small room on a daily basis, projects in all stages of development throughout the classroom, and alone-time practically nonexistent, there was little chance for my room to stay organized.

I had thirty minutes free after lunch one day, so I decided to do a little organizing. Because it was a short period of time, I chose to clean out the one small closet that was in the back of my room. While pulling bags and books out, I found a tote filled with teaching materials I had borrowed from Mrs. Cameron, a fourth grade teacher. I had deliberately put the tote on the top shelf to keep it from getting damaged but had forgotten it was there! The tote was filled with materials that I knew Mrs. Cameron would be missing. I looked up her class schedule and saw that her students were at music, so it would be a perfect time to return the tote. Since her room was close to mine, I decided to have the first student who came to class return the tote for me. Donny, a sixth grader, was that first child.

When Donny came into the room, I asked him to take the tote to Mrs. Cameron. He happily agreed to take it, but he quickly asked what he was going to get for helping me. Honestly, I thought he was kidding, so I smiled, said nothing and continued sorting through the closet. Then I noticed that he wasn't moving. I looked in his direction and saw that he had a perturbed expression on his face. When we made eye contact, he asked again what he was going to get for helping me. Hoping I was misreading his tone and physical stance, I asked him what he was talking about. With an annoyed voice, he informed me that the teacher I replaced would give the students candy, pencils, erasers, etc. for helping her in the room and inquired again what I was going to give him for helping.

As with this and many other occasions, I had to remind my students that I was not their former teacher. What she did was fine for her (not that I really believed that, but I wasn't going to speak negatively about someone the students liked). In this case, I explained that giving him something for helping me was not how I handled the same situation. I asked him again to take the tote to Mrs. Cameron, but this time he grunted out that if he wasn't going to get anything, he wasn't going to take it and proceeded to turn away!

Shocked by the pretentious and flippant attitude exuding from this child, I had to take a quick moment to compose myself. Very kindly, I agreed to give him something for helping me and amazingly those small generic words magically turned him around. I continued saying that I would actually give him two things. Now we were talking! Hearing that he would get two things, Donny even started walking toward me. When he was close, I bent down so my face was right in front of his and said that first, he would receive the utmost gratitude from me for helping and second, he would receive internal pride for doing a good deed for someone else.

I didn't even get to finish talking when he gave me a dirty look, rolled his eyes in a disgusted manner, turned around, and strutted off! This time, struggling not to lose my temper, I stood straight up and with quite an angry but quiet voice, demanded that he pick up the tote and take it to Mrs. Cameron's room immediately! I added that he better never turn his back on me or disobey me again. He slowly turned around and contemptuously glared at me. Having run out of child psychology tactics, I stomped my foot and yelled, "Now, young man!" Something must have struck a nerve because he quickly picked up the tote and hurried out the door.

I knew Donny wasn't going to be in the best of spirits when he returned, but I still felt the incident was over except for thanking him. How wrong I was! It turned out that Mrs. Cameron had been looking for her school supplies and when she saw Donny at her door with the materials, she greeted him with a huge smile and exclaimed over and over how much she appreciated him bringing it all back to her. She even gave him a hug!

While this was going on, I was in my room waiting for Donny to return. The errand should have only taken a few minutes, but it was taking much longer. Worried that Donny had decided to take advantage of his freedom outside of class, I was getting ready to go look for him. I was thrilled that I had decided to wait just a little longer because in a few minutes I heard him coming up the steps. I expected to be greeted by an angry face or maybe even a snarl but to my surprise, Donny returned with a smile! Smiling back at him, I gave him an exuberant yet suspicious, "Thank you so much for helping me!" and was totally baffled by his good mood.

Instead of going to his desk, Donny walked up to me and with a smiling face, asked if I had any other errands for him to run. Hmmm...? What was his ulterior motive? Since I was not sure about his new-found desire to help, I wanted to hear what happened with Mrs. Cameron. Without missing a beat, Donny explained how excited she had been to get her materials back, and it was obvious that he genuinely wanted to do more.

Mentally, I filtered through a handful of options for him to do where he could have another good experience. The school secretary immediately popped into my mind. Mrs. McKay was exceptionally smart and professional and though she was *just* a secretary, we all knew she was responsible for making the school run smoothly. I found it humorous that no one ever missed the principal if he was absent, but everyone knew when Mrs. McKay wasn't there because nothing seemed to get done properly. Along with running the school, she was also gooey sweet with all the children, and she wouldn't mind if I had something delivered to her. I knew she would handle Donny very well.

As he ended his tale about Mrs. Cameron giving him a hug, I told him I had some papers that needed to go to the office, and he would help me a great deal if he took them to Mrs. McKay. Energetically, he nodded his head and held out his hand. Giving him the papers, I hinted that he might not always be greeted with so much excitement as Mrs. Cameron had shown but added that I was thrilled to see he liked helping people.

Before Donny left the room, I asked him one last question about his trip to Mrs. Cameron's room. I was dying to know what took him so long but nonchalantly asked what else he did before he returned to our class. With a proud smile on his face, he said that he had offered to help empty the tote and put away all the material for Mrs. Cameron!

In the end, I actually had delivered on my promise to give Donny two things. He got my utmost appreciation for helping me and received priceless internal pride for doing a good deed for someone else!

Paddling

MY PARENTS HAVE every right to say they told me so because while I was growing up they always warned me to think before I spoke. They cautioned that if I didn't learn this crucial habit, it would catch up with me. They were right about it catching up with me, but unfortunately, it was at the expense of one of my students.

I guess Robbie and I had the same problem. Our unrestrained words backfired on us. Robbie was a fourth grader with many problems at home as well as with his learning style. He tried to cover up his emotional turmoil by having a bad attitude, and he and I were always going head to head each class period. Most days it was a real struggle getting through the time Robbie was in my class without losing my temper. He was confrontational, belligerent, disruptive, obstinate, obnoxious, and an all-around pain in the neck.

I can't remember the situation that started it all but it doesn't really matter. What unfolded was that Robbie didn't like what we were doing in class, and he literally swore in response to his agitation. I have since learned how to deal with this type of situation with control and effectiveness without making a bigger problem, but I did not know then. Still having to learn to think before I spoke, I warned Robbie that if he swore again, he would go straight to the principal's office. Literally seconds after my threat, in defiance or to save face in front of his classmates, Robbie swore again. I didn't say another word to him. I knew what I had to do, despite how senseless and ridiculously minor the offense was. To save face and my credibility, which was paramount to the success of my classroom, I had to take Robbie to the office, which meant he would be paddled. He knew it and I knew it.

As we walked to the office, I held his arm as he wriggled around pleading to get another chance. Robbie always wanted another chance. I had already given him another chance, and he blew it. I didn't speak to him or even look at him because I truly wanted to give in to his pleas, but I knew I had to follow through with my threat. I hated every step we took as we got closer to the office. Hopefully, Robbie has forgotten this event or at least the magnitude of it, but I certainly haven't. Whenever I think about this whole scenario, I know my guilt-meter skyrockets because I was an inexperienced teacher, and a child suffered for it. If I had a chance to do it all over again, I would handle this situation so differently but unfortunately, I too had been warned, and I blew it just as Robbie had.

In the office, I let Mrs. McKay know that I needed to see the principal immediately, holding onto as much composure as I could. (Now, keep in mind that I had no respect for this principal and neither did Robbie, but I turned over a very important disciplinary act to him!) When the principal came out, I told him what happened. He said he got the picture and asked if I wanted to be in his office with Robbie when he talked to him. I quickly uttered a nervous no. I couldn't bear to watch him be paddled. Sitting outside his office, I heard the principal yelling at Robbie. (Very effective, right?) Then it got quiet. The silence was broken by a popping sound. I jumped. Then another. I jumped again. Then there was silence. The lump in my throat was so large I couldn't swallow.

It seemed like an eternity before the door opened. When it did, Robbie came out first with a very red face and tears streaming down, but he was making no noise. It was obvious he was trying to keep whatever dignity he still had, and he marched right out the office, looking at no one. At this point, I didn't dare blink or I would be looking like Robbie, so I just followed him out the door.

In the hall, I wrapped my arm around him, but he was stiff as a board. My heart was breaking because of what I had done, and I silently started to cry. As we left the main building heading toward the trailer, Robbie broke down crying too.

We managed to get into the trailer before we both made a tearful scene. Fortunately for us, no one was in the trailer. We sat down and caught a glimpse of each other. We were both red faced, mad, and hurt. I think Robbie was most surprised to see me crying because he stopped for just a moment to study my face. I spoke first admitting that I was mad at him and declared that I never wanted to go through that again. I confessed that I was sorry he had to get paddled, and I reminded him that he had been given a warning, and he didn't listen. I explained that it was obvious earlier that he didn't believe I meant what I said, but maybe he learned now that I did. I told him he was the first student I ever had to have paddled, and I prayed he was my last (and thankfully, he was)!

With the largest tears streaming down his face, he actually apologized for swearing and for getting paddled. If I hadn't already been crying, I would have started then. I couldn't believe that he apologized for being paddled! Robbie promised he would not swear again in class and that he would try to talk with me when he was upset about something. We ended our talk with a simple but emotional side hug. Then redirecting the atmosphere in the room before the other students arrived, I stated that things were going to get better for both of us from here on out. And they did.

Weeks passed without any incident with Robbie. He

started coming into class willingly, and his behavior was quite tame from what it had been. Actually, he and I had a handful of occasions where we laughed and joked around. Out of the blue one day, Robbie even gave me a beautiful paperweight with the word *friend* on it.

About four months after the paddling incident, an extremely belligerent student named Alexander was placed in my room. Alexander did something that needed correcting, and I warned him not to do it again. He looked at me with laser sharp contempt, as if he was ready for a standoff. Robbie must have seen it too because he walked over to Alexander and with a friendly gesture toward me talked to him. Robbie warned him not even to try fighting with Miss Chandler because she always won. He knew from experience. He briefly explained his punishment from me. I am not sure whether Alexander thought Robbie was nuts or whether he believed him, but Robbie managed to stop him from getting in trouble.

From then on, Robbie was my unofficial discipline deputy. All new students were forewarned by him not to mess around with Miss Chandler. He promised that when I scolded, I meant it, and when I warned someone, I would follow through, so they better just do what Miss Chandler said! Not a bad spokesperson to have on my side.

Mrs. Martin

TWO MONTHS INTO my first full year teaching, I believe God decided I needed help from an earthly angel so He opened the heavens and dropped Mrs. Martin onto my doorstep. He definitely understood that I desperately needed her. I was exhausted from coming to work early and then working late into the evening preparing for classes the next day. I would work all day Saturday and Sunday many times to get an extra jump on what I needed to do for the upcoming week. Since each one of my students needed individual help, I believed their assignments needed to be individual as well, which took a great deal of time planning and creating. Taking my job and its responsibilities very seriously and not really being trained for all its demands, I became an emotional wreck. I always felt I was falling short of what my students needed, so because of my inexperience, overload of students, and pure frustration, I went searching for volunteers to help me. I knew what I wanted to accomplish in my classroom, but I couldn't physically do it by myself so there was no question; I needed help!

I never imagined that getting volunteers would have been so hard or time consuming. It was difficult enough to find a volunteer, let alone one who would be dependable, qualified, and trustworthy. As for time required of the volunteer, I wasn't asking for much. I just wanted a few volunteers, each willing to help out two to three hours a week, allowing me to offer more one-on-one attention to each of my students. I naively believed this would be easy to accomplish since I thought there would be plenty of people wanting and willing to work with children. There was a handful of people who initially were interested in working with children, but when they heard my class was for special education students, no one seemed to have the time. If I hadn't been so desperate, all the wild excuses I heard for why they couldn't help would have been hilarious. In the situation I was in, nothing seemed funny. The search went on for several weeks. I couldn't find any serious volunteers or other remedies to lessen the continued pressure I was experiencing.

Eventually, I did talk to the right person—my hairdresser! I spouted off to him, as many of his clients did. He was a good listener, but he was also a good talker. He loved to gossip. Days later, while cutting another woman's hair, he told her all about my dilemma. That woman, whom I didn't know at all, told my predicament to a friend of hers. It so happened that this friend had just lost her invalid mother and was looking for something to fill her time. This angel from heaven only knew the name of the school and that there was a teacher who needed help working with special education children. Miraculously, she was compelled to find me.

Early one morning, Mrs. McKay called me over the intercom to let me know that someone was on the phone who was interested in volunteering in my class. She gingerly asked if I wanted to take the call since she knew how cynical I had become with the whole ordeal. I really didn't hold out any hope, but I thought it would be impolite not to take the call, so I begrudgingly said I would be right there. All the way to the office, I felt like I was just wasting more of my time. At that point, I was more discouraged than ever.

After I answered the phone with a fake upbeat voice, the genuinely sweet-sounding woman on the other end introduced herself as Lois Martin and graciously asked if I still needed any help in my classroom. I restrained from uttering all the sarcastic remarks that went pouring through my head. Continuing to imitate a happy person, I replied that I did indeed still need help and robotically gave her a general overview of the children and the type of class I had. After I explained my class (which is where I lost everyone else), I was shocked to hear that she was still interested! Trying not to get overly excited, I sheepishly asked when she might be available to volunteer, assuming things worked out. She replied that mornings were better for her and literally asked if eight thirty to eleven would be all right! After I scraped myself off the floor, I quickly answered that those hours would be wonderful and inquired which day would be good for her. This woman from heaven asked if every day at the same time would be all right! I couldn't believe my ears. It was all too good to be true. I continued to ask questions knowing that something was going to pop my bubble of joy but, thankfully, nothing did.

Through our conversation, I learned that Mrs. Martin had taught various subjects abroad as she traveled with her husband, an admiral in the Navy, and her two sons. She did not have formal training as a teacher, but she had loads of experience, experience my students and I needed! I didn't think things could get any better, but I was wrong. Mrs. Martin started volunteering the next day and when she walked into my room, she brought hope, energy, determination, and a smile that stayed with my students and me for the next five years!

Worth the Wait

JUST BEFORE MRS. Martin started volunteering, she learned that she had osteoporosis. It was the same painful disease that had afflicted her mother and that eventually caused her death. Mrs. Martin promised herself that she would never let that happen to her, so she assumed direct control of her situation with a take-charge attitude. She educated herself on the disease and chose the best doctors who could help direct her medical care. Mrs. Martin was incredibly active and positive. After her treatments began, she continued to snow ski and wind surf. I am not talking about a twenty or thirty-year old. Mrs. Martin was sixty-five! I had great respect and awe for her because despite all the pain and discomfort she experienced, she never complained or missed a day working with the students and me.

Initially, there was a great deal of work for me preparing assignments for Mrs. Martin to use. Just as I did for myself, I would plan and write out everything for each particular student she helped. I soon learned that she was very creative and had wonderful teaching methods of her own, and she didn't need any of my help.

At first, Mrs. Martin only worked with a few specific

students, ones who needed the most assistance. Over time, she became so popular that all my students wanted their turn to be with her. It was seen as a real honor to be with Mrs. Martin, so the students would strive to earn the privilege to work with her. The opportunity just to be with her was such an awesome and positive motivator!

Anyone who spent time with my students found how easy it was to get personally and emotionally attached. Mrs. Martin was no different. Once she learned the academic struggles of the students, she started to create her own materials to reach particular needs. After getting to know many of the parents of the students she helped, she and her husband would take some of the students to their lake house or to the beach. For a handful of children, she and her husband became extended family members. The last time I saw Mrs. Martin was about ten years after we stopped working together when we both had been invited to the wedding of one of our students. It was quite an exciting and emotional time!

The months I struggled trying to work with my students by myself and the time I spent trying to find a volunteer seem so trivial looking back. God knew I needed Mrs. Martin, and she was worth the wait. Over the five years she volunteered, Mrs. Martin worked in the trailer on the baking hot summer days when the air conditioner didn't work and the freezing cold days when the heater didn't work. She would come on teacher-workdays when I would forget to tell her not to come. She put up with all the odd happenings that took place in our room, and she did it with a smile and a loving attitude.

There are not enough accolades to properly express how invaluable Mrs. Martin was to our class. I believe she continued with us for so many years because it was obvious she was desperately needed, and she knew she made a positive difference. Through all the struggles and challenges that she had to endure with us, I pray that she knew how much each and every one of us dearly loved her!

Whom to Count?

THE NATIONAL ACADEMIC Testing was nearing, so the preparation for it was the main conversation in the teachers' lounge. I always tried to avoid the teachers' lounge at any time, but I made sure I didn't go near it during this testing preparation period. Many of the teachers would sit around the lounge and tell all types of stories about their students and how bad their class was that year and moan about their students' grades being so low. It was obvious that they were trying to find an excuse just in case their class happened to score poorly on the national tests. When the scores would come back and maybe for the good, those same teachers were sure to take the credit. Unfortunately, on this particular day, I would have been better off tolerating the teachers in the lounge.

Trying to avoid the lounge, I went the long way to my class. As I was walking down the side hall, I heard "Hey, Chandler!" I never liked being called "Chandler" let alone "Hey, Chandler!" My name was Miss Chandler, Katherine, Kathy, or even Kath, but it was not "Hey, Chandler!" There was only one person at the school who was rude enough to address me that way, and that was the principal.

I know I have already talked about this man and how he

was just a ladder climber and not interested in my students at all, but let me describe him now. He was about five feet six inches tall. He had dyed golden-blond hair that was combed back using some type of glossy gel. His face was large, puffy, and reddish. He had a double chin and was probably forty or so pounds overweight. He was a perfectionist when it came to clothing since everything matched and nothing was ever out of place. Then to complete his persona, there was his gait, which was abrupt and somewhat like a bulldozer.

I am the type of person who has a wide, and I mean wide, personal space, and he was one of those people who had a very narrow personal space. This was not a good combination since I had absolutely no respect for this man at all. On this particular occasion, as well as others, he started talking to me standing just inches from me and was so close I could feel his breath when he spoke. This was way too close, so I started inching away from him but he kept moving forward, back into my space. I tried to pay attention to what he was saying, but I was still irritated by how he had addressed me, and instinctually I was trying to keep my distance, so what he was saying really didn't interest me.

When I finally heard what he was saying, I was not sure what made me angrier: his egocentric view or his arrogance. Actually, it was probably a combination of both. He said he wanted to see how I could work my schedule so I could keep my students in my class during the national testing sessions. What he thought he had figured out was that if my students were in my room, they could be counted absent from the testing sessions! I couldn't believe this man wanted to manipulate the lower-functioning students to keep his school's overall average up. That was the ego viewpoint. He showed no interest in finding the school's real scores so he could learn where improvements were needed. Forget how the school was actually functioning; he just wanted to look good and climb that educational administration ladder.

The ridiculousness of his position showed up when he thought the few students I had who actually would perform poorly on these national tests would affect the classroom or the school's overall average. It just showed that he had no idea who my students were and what their academic challenges were. Most of my students were average or above average in one or more areas of study. He didn't realize that most of my students might score poorly in one area of study but then on other parts of the testing, score as well or better than the other students in their class.

I stopped listening to him bluster about how I could keep my students in my room because I was mentally recalling the conversation he had with me about a month earlier. Due to federal and state requirements, this same man had asked me to give a head count of all the students I was servicing. The number of special education students would determine how much funding we would receive, and he wanted to make sure we counted absolutely every possible child. After I had given him my number, he vehemently disagreed and requested that I come to his office with the list of my students so we could scour over the names together to see if I might have missed someone. He repeatedly poured over my list, unsuccessful at finding any other student to count. With this situation still crystal clear in my memory, this man was now standing in front of me, breathing on me, trying to sweep my students under a rug, and not count them this time around.

I tuned back to his monologue when I heard him ask, "What do you think?" I looked at him and bluntly said, "I believe if you count my students for money, you had better count my students for testing. I have a class I need to get back to. Please excuse me." There was nothing else to say, so I just walked away.

This was the only confrontation we ever had, if you were even to call it that, but from that point on, this man was a bit colder and ruder to me. I didn't really care because I knew I had no support from him in regard to my class anyway, so I worked hard to avoid him as much as possible.

It was sad that I felt I had to avoid him because a principal can be such a positive influence for the entire school. Since my experience with this principal, I have had the privilege to work for excellent principals who did wonders for the teachers, school, and most importantly, the students. Regarding this particular principal, I guess I shouldn't have expected so much from someone who called me "Hey, Chandler."

Colton

COLTON WAS A beautiful child. He had a flawless complexion with the warmest dark brown eyes and curly, dark brown hair. He had a slender build and was small overall for being six years old and in the first grade. Colton came from a loving and hardworking family. It was obvious both parents took a great deal of time to work with him. He was definitely actively loved.

Colton was intrigued by life and the situations it brought. He was always trying to find answers to what he was seeing and experiencing, so his questions were never ending. His personality was quirky but genuine. Colton's inner charm was equal to or better than his outer appearance. He was gentle, kind, caring, and thoughtful. In my opinion, everything about him was perfect.

One of his quirky traits was when he walked. His gait was always with great intention. I knew it wasn't true, but it seemed as if Colton couldn't walk and talk at the same time. He would be headstrong to walk somewhere in the room and stop halfway to wherever he was headed to say something or ask a question. When he finished what he had to say, he resumed walking, concentrating on his destination.

Another interesting trait of Colton's was that the little motor inside his body wouldn't slow down long enough for him to sit for even a few minutes. That made it hard for him to do his schoolwork and was one of the reasons he was in my class. As with many of my students, I had to prioritize what I really wanted to teach. With Colton, I had to ask myself if I wanted him to learn the material I had to offer him, or if I want him to learn how to sit in his seat. This was an easy decision. Colton, and only Colton, was allowed to walk a route in the trailer. By allowing him to do this, he was able to read as he walked around and around the room. Permitting him to do this presented a slight problem: he couldn't see where he was going while he was walking and reading. At first, I solved this problem by pulling all the furniture away from the walls, making a clear path that allowed Colton an easy no-obstruction route to follow. This solution also gave him the protection and safety of the walls, which he seemed to need. As his confidence grew, the furniture was left where it belonged, so that meant the other students and I had to make sure nothing was in his chosen path or he was sure to trip. If he needed to write something while he was walking around, he'd stop, use the nearest desk, and then continue walking. The students had learned that every one of them got different *special* privileges so no one ever complained or caused any problems with Colton's walks or his use of their desks. If anything, they all worked very hard to keep things out of his way because they didn't want him to get hurt.

With his constant search for answers, life in general was very serious for Colton. When he first started in my room, he was nervous and rarely said anything. After more than a year, he loosened up a bit and started showing off his wonderful dry sense of humor. I believe a person has to have a deep understanding of concepts to be able to show a good dry sense of humor. Though he eventually revealed his wonderful humor, he and I had some thick walls to break down before we all got to experience and enjoy Colton's humor. In addition to his serious state of mind and active body, Colton suffered from being exceptionally sensitive and self-conscience. With his emotions magnified, life seemed even harder for him. Getting to and from class was a struggle. Sitting next to a new student was a struggle. Finding his books was a struggle. Seeing his shoe was untied was a struggle. Having a new schedule to follow due to an assembly was a struggle. Everything seemed to be a struggle for Colton.

With all of my students, I worked very hard to uphold high academic standards, but I also tried to keep things light with the mood in the room since we were always dealing with very stressful academic and emotional issues. I would joke around with my students and use my lovable, furry hand puppets to keep things new and fun. Every one of my students loved the puppets and my clowning around except for Colton. He didn't like any of it! He couldn't tolerate any joking and didn't seem to understand the purpose for puppets. He would push them away and say over and over that they weren't real and demand that I put them down.

It was sad, but I eventually learned that I couldn't joke or play around with him because his response to any kidding was always awkward and sometimes even seemed painful for him to endure. My efforts to have fun with Colton only led to tears filling his eyes. There was nothing more painful than to see Colton holding back huge tears. Because of his extreme reaction, the other students and I backed off from goofing around when Colton was in the room. I hurt for him, but I knew that when he was ready, if ever, we would welcome him into the fun.

Early on, working with Colton was quite a challenge because he wouldn't look at me. Instead of looking at me when I was talking to him, he would look in the direction of my ear. For some reason that habit drove me crazy. It wasn't that he avoided eye contact with me. He couldn't seem to make eye contact with anyone. When the time came, after many months being in my room, I felt I could have *a little* fun with him. Every time Colton looked at my ear, I would move my face in his line of vision. He immediately moved his eyes somewhere other than my face, maybe would give me a slight smile, and then would ask what I was doing. Though I was consistent with my response to him looking at my ear and not my face, his response was equally consistent. I couldn't seem to get him to fix his eyes on my face. On days when my patience was thin and his gazing at my ear would get the best of me, I would gently hold his face toward mine, but all he would do was close his eyes and smile! I just couldn't win getting him to look at me but at least I'd get a smile!

The wonderful outcome for Colton was that over time, as he became more self-assured, he was able to look at people during a conversation, walk with confidence, and sit still for longer and longer periods of time. Interestingly, it was only when Colton was ready that those achievements occurred.

Colton's Butterfly

I COULD SEE Colton becoming a doctor, researcher, or someone dealing with science questions and finding their answers. I had never seen a child as young as he was so enthralled in science-oriented topics and filled with such well thought out intriguing and deep questions. I had thought I was fairly smart until Colton started asking questions, and I rarely could give any answer without having to seek out details that he seemed to need. I certainly learned a great deal from him through the years with all his questions.

One day, Colton and I were walking outside together headed toward the trailer. Walking with Colton was always an adventure. He usually walked with his head down or tilted up, rarely looking straight ahead. He was too busy seeing all the wonders of the world to worry about the mundane man-made objects he could run into. On this particular day, Colton was walking with his head down, and he spotted a very large, dead butterfly. I knew it was dead right away because it just had that dead butterfly look to it. Colton didn't agree. He stooped down to touch the butterfly and was surprised when it didn't fly away. He nudged it again. Then he turned to me with the most puzzled look and asked what was wrong with the butterfly. To me, it was obvious, and I was surprised by his lack of understanding of the creature's dilemma. The butterfly was just plain dead! I forgot that nothing was simple with Colton. Details and more details were always in demand. I gently said that I thought the butterfly was dead. Interrupting my further explanation, Colton disagreed. He disagreed in a very matter of fact way and not in a rude or disrespectful way, but it was just that I was wrong, and he seemed surprised by my lack of understanding of the creature's situation. He told me, in the most confident tone, that the butterfly couldn't be dead because it was still so colorful! What a marvelous observation and conclusion. I agreed with him that it was colorful but said again that the butterfly was no longer alive. Colton stuck to his guns and continued to support his opinion by letting me know that when people died, their skin changed color rapidly. Arthropods would certainly turn pale faster than humans since they had shorter life spans and were much smaller. Remember, this is a six-year-old!

I wasn't getting anywhere with logic or rather with my type of logic, because who could argue with Colton's reasoning? I changed gears with him and offered to get a glass jar to put the butterfly in it so we could observe it in the classroom. Again, he looked at me like I was crazy. He explained that he didn't want to move the butterfly because its family wouldn't know where it was, and they might worry. With this line of thinking, I conceded and suggested that every so often, during his class time with me, he could check on the butterfly to see how it was doing. Thankfully, he liked the idea.

Each time Colton came back from visiting the butterfly, he was more and more confused because it was still there and still not moving. After the fifth visit, he finally agreed that the butterfly was dead but wanted to understand why it was still so colorful. I praised him for his persistence in wanting to find an acceptable answer and apologized that none of my explanations satisfied him. I did say that I knew one thing for sure and that was that God meant the butterfly to stay colorful even though it was dead. Then I added that I was certain that one day he would find someone more capable of giving him the answer he deserved.

For some reason, that explanation satisfied him.

A Green Pendant

THERE WAS A change in the free/reduced lunch program at our school and by the reaction of some parents, one might have thought the world was coming to an end. I had heard from the office personnel that they had been flooded with phone calls from parents angry at the unreasonable changes that had been made. Originally, families who qualified for special lunches were either getting the lunches for free or they were being charged twenty-five cents per meal, while other families were paying the full price of a dollar and twenty-five cents. The change that caused such an outrage from the parents of the children receiving free/reduced lunches was that they were now going to have to pay five cents more a meal. That meant the free lunches were now five cents and the reduced lunches were now thirty cents. Keep in mind that the other parents who were not on any special lunch program now had to pay one dollar and fifty cents: a twenty-five-cent increase per day. There were a few calls from the latter parents, but the vast majority of phone calls came from the parents of the special lunch program, and they were outraged at the injustice being dealt them.

Other than believing these parents were very spoiled

with the reduced lunch program as it was, I really didn't think too much of the overall situation. To me, it was absolutely depressing to hear these parents complain so vehemently, when all they had to do was to pay twenty-five cents total or pay an additional twenty-five cents per week for their child to be fed a healthy and tasty meal. The power of entitlement resounded with their reactions. I never realized that the problem went much deeper than with just the parents until one day while in the lunch line a seven-year old opened my eyes to the real harm that was being done.

In our school, students who got free or reduced lunches were given a yarn necklace with a laminated piece of construction paper as a pendant to wear when they entered the lunch line. Green meant the child got lunch for free and blue meant the child received a reduced lunch. This method, though not perfect and years before the technology that could help with this situation, let the cashier know who paid what amount quickly so the children could move smoothly through the line.

On this particular day, I had not brought my lunch so I went to the cafeteria to buy my meal. I stood in line behind a first grade class and the last student in line was a boy named Henry. I tried to engage in a conversation with him but the line was moving so fast, we didn't have much time to talk. With lunch trays in hand, we were by the register in no time. The cashier held out her hand for the nickel Henry owed her. You see, he had on a green pendant. Henry didn't notice her hand and walked off with his tray, as I would guess he had done for most, if not all, of his school lunches. The cashier called for him to come back, but Henry only turned around and gave her an impatient and confused look. The woman kindly said that he owed her a nickel. Henry quickly held up his green pendant as if it were a trophy and said his lunch was free. Oops! No one must have told Henry about the change in price. The cashier explained very nicely that his lunch was now a nickel.

This young child's whole demeanor changed as if he were part chameleon. His once happy-go-lucky, child-like personality turned belligerent and rude. He stood there and stared at her indignantly. What he said next is what all adults should hear to understand what our educational and governmental systems are teaching our young people. He said arrogantly, with his foot tapping and one hand on his hip that nobody worked at his house, so he got things free!

All the book knowledge in the world means nothing if this is what our children learn about life and themselves: if they don't work, they get rewarded! No pride, no sense of responsibility. What a waste!

Samantha

SAMANTHA WAS LIKE the vast majority of my students; she looked quite *normal*. She was a beautiful seven-year old who was in the first grade. She had the shiniest white blonde hair with very fair skin and the most beautiful blue eyes. Though she was absolutely adorable, her overall appearance disguised the academic and behavioral struggles Samantha had to deal with on a daily basis. Another problem, unique to Samantha, only showed up if she was asked to talk. In short, she just plain wouldn't! When asked to say something, she would hide or vehemently shake her head. If she was with people she felt comfortable with, she would utter grunts or words in a non-sensical order and only her parents, older brother, and a few select friends would be able to interpret her garbled words.

Prior to Samantha coming to our school, the previous school's teacher had convinced the parents to retain Samantha due to her diagnosed learning disabilities. Along with being labeled learning disabled and having a serious speech problem, Samantha was also diagnosed as hyperactive. Samantha definitely had problems, but I didn't agree with all of the recommended treatments the medical professionals had prescribed.

With her challenges, Samantha's situation was magnified by the fact that her older brother seemed to be flawless. He was good looking, outgoing, kind, mannerly, athletic, musical, and impressively modest. He was also extremely smart and qualified to attend the gifted and talented program. Though Samantha's parents tried very hard not to compare the two siblings, Samantha was not blind to the vast differences between the two of them. She saw that her brother outshined her, and it seemed to make her coil into her shell even more.

Samantha was one of the most challenging students I ever taught. Teachers are people who want to help students, and we thrive on seeing improvements in them. But it is a two-way street. The old adage "You can lead a horse to water, but you can't make it drink" perfectly describes the situation with Samantha. She had dedicated professionals and a loving family right there to help her, yet she just refused to do anything to help herself.

At school, I was privileged to work with many talented teachers. One was the speech teacher, Mrs. Taylor. She was one of my favorite teachers to work with because she was a sweet-spirited woman who worked hard, loved her students, loved her job, and was quite successful at it. Though we had tight quarters, I was fortunate to share the trailer with her for three years, allowing me the opportunity to witness the many advances she achieved with her students. She was amazing.

As capable as Mrs. Taylor was, she was not seeing any significant improvement with Samantha either. Being discouraged herself, Mrs. Taylor decided to teach both Samantha's regular classroom teacher and me the same techniques and methods she was using so Samantha would have consistency with all of her instruction and interaction.

I can't speak for the other teachers but even with all the extra support we gave each other, I quickly got fed up with Samantha's grunts and shaking of her head refusing to do whatever I asked her to do. My formal responsibility with

Samantha was to work with her academically. Specifically, I was to help her with her reading and math, but I couldn't figure out how to do that if she wouldn't even talk to me. Plus, while working with her reading and math skills, I had to deal with her hyperactivity. I felt like a complete failure because I couldn't seem to get anywhere with her.

Months went by and still there was no significant sign of improvement in any area with Samantha. Something was wrong. We were missing a crucial piece to this puzzling situation. Purely by accident, I stumbled onto one of the roots of our problem. It happened in the cafeteria during lunch.

It was always my preference to eat lunch in my room, but whenever I was invited by a student to have lunch with them, I always accepted. I had never liked the cafeteria as a child, and I really didn't like it as an adult, but it was a great place to get to know my students better, and I truly enjoyed spending time with them and their friends.

One particular occasion, Samantha asked, in her garbled way, if I would have lunch with her. I was thrilled that she invited me so I enthusiastically accepted. With a huge smile on her face, she immediately grabbed my hand and began hopping and skipping toward the cafeteria, pulling me as I tried keeping up with her fast gait. In the cafeteria, she pointed at the chair I was to sit in. Not wanting to cause a problem in front of her classmates, I just sat down. We sat with three of her friends from her regular classroom and it was there I found some of the missing pieces to our puzzling struggles with Samantha.

Samantha never had to say a word. Her friends were so *in tune* with her that she rarely ever had to utter a sound let alone a word. Her eyes and the slightest tilt of her head were all she had to display to get help. Without saying a word, one girl passed the salt to Samantha and then one girl went to get an extra spoon for Samantha when her spoon fell. I was amazed to hear Samantha actually talk a little, but the three girls would fill in or complete Samantha's sentences when she got stuck. There was no effort or struggle in the girls' interactions. It was fluid and happy. Actually, it was awesome to see this precious outlay of friendship. Samantha's friends seemed to know exactly what she needed and they were waiting on her as if she were a queen.

What I had to do now was to teach her friends how to help Samantha talk for herself. I could tell they already wanted to help; I just needed to show them another way of helping. With Samantha's full knowledge of my plan, the girls were thrilled at the invitation to become speech deputies for their friend. I worked out several times for these girls to come to my room during school, with their parents' permission, to learn some of the basic techniques Mrs. Taylor had taught me to work with Samantha. I made sure what I asked them to do was simple and fun because I never wanted to hurt their friendship with Samantha. My goal with these girls was to keep Samantha from becoming lazy or spoiled by having her friends do all her talking. Maybe it was purely a coincidence but shortly after her friends started helping, Samantha began showing a little more progress with her willingness to talk. Samantha continued to struggle with some areas regarding her speech, but she eventually became more willing to help herself, and that is when we finally started to see some real progress.

My next hurdle with Samantha was her hyperactivity. Because her parents and the medical professionals believed Samantha suffered from extreme hyperactivity, she was given high doses of Ritalin. I absolutely hate the use of this drug and the other behavior-altering drugs to manipulate a child's behavior. I especially hate it when little to nothing else is tried before drugs are prescribed. Prescribing behavior-altering drugs is such an easy fix for the parents, the school, and the medical professionals yet so many times drugs probably wouldn't even be needed if a few life-style changes would be tried. It is my belief that proper regular sleep, a whole food diet, consistent routine, limited use of technology, regular exercise, and a loving home environment are just a few of the obvious factors that need to be in a child's life for a long period of time before even thinking of using mood-altering drugs.

I could always tell when Samantha was on her prescribed drugs because she was almost unable to function. She hardly moved. I could also tell when the drug was wearing off because she would start bouncing all around having great difficulty sitting, let alone sitting still. Her moods and behavior were like riding a roller coaster day after day. If I was confused and frustrated with her behavioral swings, I couldn't begin to imagine what she was going through.

One of the many side effects of using Ritalin was that Samantha never grew. Over the first year I worked with her, she didn't grow any or gain weight at all. The pediatrician assured her parents there was nothing to worry about since over the summer, she would take Samantha off the Ritalin, allowing her to "catch up" with her growth and weight gain. She explained that in clinical trials this method was found to be successful. Unfortunately, this theory may have sounded good, but it didn't work. Summer came and went and Samantha had gained no weight or height.

Mrs. Taylor and I met with the parents at the end of the first summer and convinced them to seek a second opinion. This doctor was alarmed by Samantha's lack of growth so he switched her medication to Cylert. This drug didn't affect her growth anymore, and Samantha didn't show as many extreme ups and downs. Regardless of these so-called improvements, I was never convinced she needed either of these drugs. Regrettably, I was unable to convince the parents to try lifestyle changes. They were convinced the lifestyle changes wouldn't help, but they did admit that offering regular sleep hours, serving a whole food diet, and insuring regular exercise would be impossible to implement since their schedules were so busy. It was obvious, though they loved their daughter, the drug was a better solution *for them.*

The slight progress Samantha achieved over the years was seen as a success by the school officials and pediatric specialists. The checkmarks may have looked good on their paperwork, but the teachers and I, who worked one-on-one with Samantha, knew differently. Sadly, Samantha and her parents were in for a long and grueling uphill battle. I believe the parents were the real root of Samantha's problems. They loved Samantha, and they wanted the best for her, but they also wanted the problem fixed with as little effort and interruption to their lives as possible. They had the money to pay for the prescriptions, and they relied on the professionals to tell them what to do. The drug offered a temporary quick-fix, but without other changes in her lifestyle, there was no real improvement. It was quite a depressing situation.

Through my challenges with Samantha, I did learn that the real successes students achieved were when parents got involved, took responsibility, and led in the care and education of their children. Parents have to follow their instincts and keep searching and educating themselves for the best direction and solutions for their child's situation, whatever that may be.

The next two stories are perfect examples of how strong parents need to be and how far they might have to go to do what is right for their child. (And it wasn't convenient for them at all!)

Retention

IT WAS AN exciting time for Colton. At least that's how all the teachers and his parents made it seem on his first day in second grade. Colton's first grade teacher, the counselor, his parents, and I all knew the road for him in second grade would be rough, but we had no idea how difficult. The teachers and I had recommended retention at the end of the first grade, but his parents refused to allow it, so everyone involved with Colton at school created various types of support to assist him as he went into the second grade.

Unfortunately, the first day in second grade didn't go well at all for Colton because he couldn't do much of the work and emotionally, he was frightened of all the new routines. Knowing that Colton would have some obvious difficulties, Mrs. Furman, his classroom teacher, and I decided to meet at the end of each day so we could discuss issues from that day and see what we could do to make the next day better. At first, we felt Colton just needed time to adjust, but with each passing day, the problems and concerns kept mounting. Worst of all, with each day, Colton seemed to suffer more and more.

My sweet, precious Colton was experiencing extreme challenges. Mrs. Furman and I witnessed him withdraw emotionally, and we knew something had to change. On day five, Mrs. Furman and I discussed every possible option. There was only one obvious solution, so we talked with the principle, the counselor, and the other special education teachers at the school, knowing we needed their support. Realizing the severity of Colton's situation, as unusual as it was, we knew he needed to be placed *back* in first grade!

On the sixth day, we met with his mother, Mrs. Cline. We explained all the issues and concerns we had for Colton and told her our proposed solution. She admitted that she and her husband were also worried about their son and what he had had to deal with in only six days. We all knew advancing to second grade would be academically difficult, but what we didn't and couldn't have foreseen was Colton's extreme and painful emotional response. He was just plain not ready for the demands of second grade. Initially, Mrs. Cline and her husband were adamantly opposed to retention, but this time around, Mrs. Cline agreed readily and willingly.

Retention is a controversial, difficult, and emotional option in any situation, let alone trying to do it after six days in a higher grade. Fortunately for Colton, his parents were supportive of both him and the school. We impressed upon Mrs. Cline the importance of her fully agreeing with this decision. She and her husband had to agree to it; their friends and relatives had to support it, and they all had to believe this was the right action to take and the correct grade for Colton. We warned that mumbled comments from anyone important to him or overheard conversations could jeopardize the success of this change. Colton was exceedingly sensitive, and the reactions of the people around him could make or break the success of retention at this point.

On the ninth day of school, Colton went back to the first grade. He was going to another first grade class, but he obviously knew what was happening. How confusing it must have been for him because now we were telling him how exciting it would be to be in the first grade and all the wonderful things he would be doing in that grade. This horrible situation would have been bewildering for any child but because of Colton's sensitivity to change, this was a nightmare.

All of the first grade teachers were phenomenal, but we chose to place Colton with Mrs. Halsted, who was perfect for him. We felt her lively but well-organized class would fit with Colton's personality, and she could help ease a bit of the immense pressure he was going to have to endure moving back to first grade.

The first day Colton was with Mrs. Halsted I waited until after lunch to ask her how he was doing. She told me that he cried all morning and now he was just silent, sitting all alone. What horrible news! Over the past nine days, I had labored over this problem and its solution, and I was hoping (and very much needed) to hear some good news. I desperately wanted to hear and see some evidence that we had made the right decision. In my head, I knew retention was the best decision, but right then my heart was breaking with the thought that I had been part of causing so much despair for my precious Colton.

When Colton came into my room that afternoon, he was definitely quieter than his already quiet personality. After I got the other students working on their lessons, I pulled him aside and talked with him about the first and second grade classes and why the changes were made. He just stared ahead, never saying much, and his eyes filled with tears. It was obvious he was not happy with either situation and was hurting inside. It was so painful to watch this beautiful child struggle with all we had dealt him.

The next day, I checked on him in the morning. He was crying again! The guilt, the doubt, and the absolute emotional pain I was experiencing around this situation were consuming all my thoughts and energy. These were some of the longest days of my teaching career. I can't imagine what they were like for Colton or for his parents!

Amazingly, on the eleventh day of school but the third day in first grade for Colton, he shed no tears, seemed a bit happier, and was warming up to his teacher and his new classmates. By the end of the day, he had successfully completed his work and actively participated in his regular class activities! We all needed these signs of improvement to let us know we had made the right decision. We may have gone the long and excruciatingly painful way to get there, but Colton was where he was supposed to be. He had a truly successful second time around in first grade, thanks to the love and support he got from his parents and the school.

The final reward came years later when I ran into Mrs. Cline at the mall. We hadn't seen each other since Colton left elementary school so she had a great deal to tell me. Mrs. Cline was delighted to let me know that when Colton completed the sixth grade, he was totally removed from any special education assistance and placed in full-time regular classrooms. She continued telling me that he completed middle school earning A and B grades!

Since I had taught him for five years, Mrs. Cline knew I would be thrilled with the outcome, and she graciously thanked me for all that the school and I had done to help Colton be happy and successful in school. She said she knew I had been instrumental in so much of his elementary school years and thanked me personally for the energy and effort I had given to guide her husband and her along with Colton.

Without question, teachers need to be paid more for all that they do, but at that moment, no amount of money could replace the incredible joy and satisfaction I was feeling. I had made a long-term positive difference in someone's future! Life just doesn't get any better than that!

Retention or Maybe Not!

RICHARD AND COLTON were in the first grade at the same time but not in the same class. Both of their teachers were exemplary professionals, and they worked very hard with the boys and with my program to achieve as much progress as possible. At the end of the year, both teachers and I recommended retention, having solid reasons for these decisions. Despite the logical reasoning we gave the parents for retention, Mr. and Mrs. Cline and Mrs. Mullen didn't agree, so both boys went on to second grade. You have just read what happened to Colton and his results. Now for what happened with Richard.

Academically, Richard was much farther behind than Colton, but he was bigger, stronger, and street smart. He was just as sweet as Colton, but he definitely knew how to fend for himself. If I ever had a teacher's pet, Richard would have been mine. He drove me crazy with all his antics and shenanigans in my class, but there was something about him that stole my heart. Richard was very protective of his classmates and me. He was always there to lend a helping hand, solve a problem, or set me straight on how things should be with the many difficult situations that would occur in my room. If his personality didn't steal my heart, his deep crevassed dimples would get me every time he smiled. I don't think anyone would have suspected or accused Richard of being a teacher's pet though because I was harder on him and expected more out of him than any other student I taught.

Richard had the privilege of having an outstanding mother. He was her only child, and she was a single mom. Over the five years I worked with Richard, I heard nothing and knew nothing about his dad. There was no mention of the father in any of Richard's records and I never inquired. There was no need to know that information since Mrs. Mullen was a dynamic mom and was doing a wonderful job with Richard on her own.

Mrs. Mullen was always well dressed, well spoken, had a good sense of humor, and carried herself with great confidence. She worked at one of the larger department stores, but I never knew in what capacity. All I knew was that she was reliable and punctual to all conferences and school meetings and diligently helped Richard with his homework. Anyone could tell her son was her pride and joy and, to some degree, her life.

At the end of first grade, I was going to have to talk with Mrs. Mullen about the need to retain Richard. Richard's maturity was normal for his age, but his reading and writing skills were that of a kindergartener. Before speaking with Mrs. Mullen, I garnered support from the School Based Committee, a committee made up of teachers from our school with various experience, to help with student placement decisions. After their review, it was concluded that Richard would best be served remaining in first grade. Because of my position as the resource teacher, I had the responsibility to meet with Mrs. Mullen and explain our recommendation. I was aware that this idea would be difficult for her to hear, but I truly believed it was the right choice for Richard, and I just knew she would agree.

As with all our other conferences, Mrs. Mullen was respectful and pleasant, but when I told her about the recommendation for retention, she would not even consider it. I tried to describe what Richard would face going on to the next grade and how much harder each grade would get thereafter. I explained that retention in later years was much harder, less productive, and in some cases, more detrimental, so now was the optimal time for helping him catch up. But Mrs. Mullen felt retention, even in the first grade, would be detrimental for her son.

Seeing I was getting nowhere, I then described to her what would have to be done to *maybe* get Richard through second grade and possibly third. I showed her some of the curriculum of the up-coming years. With each grade, there was more and more material to be covered so there wasn't much room for catch-up time. I explained that I could *officially* increase the time Richard came to work with me, but she knew he was already working with me *unofficially* more than the allowable amount of time per day for a resource placement.

I told her my goal for Richard was to need me less and less but unfortunately, without retention, he would need me more and more. Whether he was retained or not, he would need her help at home to keep him progressing. Without retention, I told her the demands on her to get Richard through each grade would be vast and ongoing. I drew a picture for her of what she would need to do with Richard over the next year and the years following. I explained that the school would do whatever it could to help Richard, but she would have the bulk of the time with him in the evenings and weekends. Nothing I said made her second-guess her decision for a moment. She just seemed more resolved and said she would do whatever it took to help her son. As usual, our conference ended on a very positive note, and she seemed to genuinely thank me for all that I was doing with and for Richard. She said she appreciated my desire to help him but in regard to retention, it just wasn't an option.

When she left, I realized I was exhausted! I was emotionally drained from all my efforts to help Mrs. Mullen see what Richard needed. I couldn't understand why she would do this to him, and I felt it was so unfair because from *my* view, Richard's future looked so bleak at such a young age. I was also upset with her for not opening her eyes to reality and seeing what was best for her son. Well, I was the one who should have had my eyes opened. The next year and the following three years Richard was at the school, Mrs. Mullen did wonders with her son. The school, as a team, gave as much assistance as possible, but it came down to Mrs. Mullen being the one to pull Richard through.

Over those four years, Richard stayed at the maximum hours allowed in my room and was always struggling in his classes. Despite the hardships he encountered, he continued to love school, love learning, work hard, use his sense of humor, smile, and find good friends. At the end of every school year, the school body would gather in the gymnasium where teachers from all the grades would hand out special awards. Amazingly, when Richard was in the fifth grade, his classroom teacher recognized all his hard work and successes and gave him her *Most Improved* award. In front of the whole school and with his mother in attendance, he walked so proudly to accept his award showing off his handsome smile and his deep crevassed dimples. As he accepted his award, no one in the gymnasium could miss the smile on Mrs. Mullen's face, beaming with love and admiration for her precious son.

Through those hard years, just maybe Mrs. Mullen knew her son better than anyone else. Maybe she knew and accepted that he would be *slow* and retention would make no difference to her son being able to ever *catch up*. Maybe what he needed was all the love, support, and positive direction that she gave to keep him on the right track for life. For me, the most wonderful part of working with Richard over the years was witnessing a young man grow to love and respect his mother, if it was even possible, more than he did before.

The final decisions regarding retention were different for Colton and Richard and yet each decision was correct. Interestingly, most of the factors involved with the decision to retain or not were the same: hard working boys, an eagerness to learn, supportive school, and dedicated teachers. The *deciding* factor for success was with the parents. In each case, the parents looked at their child, saw what was needed and then did *whatever* it took to help their child succeed. Yes, I said it: The parents! This concept seems to be difficult for some parents to accept, but parents, and only parents, are ultimately responsible for their child's success in school. This is even truer today since there are many options other than just traditional public schools and church schools. As parents, it is *our* job and *our* responsibility to learn what *our* child needs and then do whatever it takes to make it happen so he or she can be as successful as possible. Just imagine what our schools would be like and the progress our children would make if more parents were as dedicated to their children and school as Mr. and Mrs. Cline and Mrs. Mullen were.

Ronald

I ALWAYS STRUGGLED with the battle of labeling students. The labels that were given to the students I worked with were to help facilitate their academic and emotional assistance. On one hand, we needed labels to identify students' needs and then offer them instruction or classrooms best suited for those needs. On the other hand, labels were just that, labels. None were good labels either. Because labels were and are so distasteful, they keep changing. In this time period, the label EMR was used for students who were having significant troubles with the majority, if not all, of their academics and social skills. These students also would exhibit difficulties with day-to-day activities. EMR was the acronym for *educable mentally retarded* and carried a horrible connotation, but that was the term that the schools used.

In the special education world, there were several classroom situations offered to students. The two most common were resource classrooms like mine where students came in for short periods of time each day to receive specific help in certain academic areas. Then there were self-contained classrooms. Students in these classrooms would stay with one teacher and a teacher's aide all day. These classrooms were limited to maybe five to eight students because they required a great deal of individual attention. If a child was labeled mildly EMR, they would be placed in my room ... that is, unless they were waiting to be placed in a self-contained class.

A precious third grader named Ronald Wade was in my room only about eight months while he waited to be placed in an EMR self-contained class. Personally, I would have loved to have had him stay with me because he worked so hard, was very mannerly, and was so much fun to be with, in or out of class. Unfortunately, he struggled with practically every facet of academics and basic life skills so he needed more than my program could offer him. I thoroughly enjoyed my eight months with him though.

As with Samantha, I recognized the opportunity to learn more about my students by eating with them, but the real reason I would cave and accept the many invitations was because I couldn't bear to see their disappointed faces. I may not have gotten a respite from the noise and confusion of the day, but I always loved my time with my students.

Ronald was one of my students who constantly invited me to sit with him. He was an absolute delight. I thoroughly enjoyed my lunches with him because he would entertain all who sat at his table with his creative and colorful stories and jokes. At the table, he would get so involved with his stories or jokes, he would forget to eat. When he did eat, he would eat in a painfully slow and methodical manner so that many days he wouldn't even eat half of his lunch. (A quick side bar to this story is that it was obvious that Ronald managed to eat at some point because he was at least ten to fifteen pounds overweight for a ten-year old.)

The jokes or stories that Ronald would tell were typical of this one:

Once upon a time, a little boy got locked in a closet. He pushed and he shoved with all his might, but he couldn't budge the door. The only thing he found in the closet was a baseball bat. He picked it up. He struck once at the door, he struck twice, he struck three times and he was out!

Oh, did Ronald laugh. He excitedly inquired if we all got it. While he was laughing, he would give a summary version of the joke: He struck once, twice, three times and was out! Then he asked again if we understood it. Even though we were all laughing, he would continue to repeat the joke as if our response wasn't quite as grand as he wanted.

One time his humor or insight showed up and he didn't even know it. I had been having many frustrating days with the administration and with my students. My tolerance was nil, and my patience was long gone. My classes were all jumbled one afternoon, and I ended up with too many students in my very small trailer. The lack of space was challenging, but the worst part was that my students seemed to forget the rules of the room and even how to think for themselves.

The condition of my room was also driving me crazy, so that added to the chaos. It may have been an icy, cold winter day outside but our heater was working too well so we had our windows open. Coats, jackets, mittens, books, melting ice, and kids were everywhere.

Along with all the confusion, it seemed as if everyone was asking for my help at the same time. I tried to fabricate tolerance, but that wasn't working. Maybe things weren't as bad as they seemed to me, but I finally snapped.

I picked up a book, slammed it on the table and demanded silence. That got everyone's attention, and they definitely got quiet immediately. I demanded that no one, absolutely no one, was allowed to utter the words "Miss Chandler" for at least the next ten minutes. Calming down just a bit, I explained that they all had been helped in one way or another and ten minutes wasn't too much to ask. I repeated myself like a broken record, hoping my request would sink in. I had my hand up in the air waving it like I had control, which I didn't, shaking it at everyone, threatening to all watching. Not a word was uttered when I finished. Faces were all glued on me. I'm not sure whether it was because they were frightened with the thought that their teacher had lost it, or they were refraining from laughing at the spectacle I made of myself. It didn't matter why because the silence was short-lived.

No sooner had I repeated that I didn't want the words "Miss Chandler" uttered, I felt a tug at my elbow. I turned around to find Ronald at my elbow, which was still semi-bent in a threatening pose. When he caught my eye, he genuinely and sincerely, asked, "Kathy, would you help me with my math problem?" Needless to say, we all broke down laughing. I needed the laughter more than the ten minutes of silence to get me back on track.

While enjoying the laughter, I noticed that Ronald wasn't laughing. He was smiling, though in a bewildered way, as if he didn't know what was funny. He looked at me again and asked, "Well, will you help me?" I realized he had no idea what quick wit or problem-solving skills he had just used. He just wanted help with his math, and he made darn sure he didn't say "Miss Chandler!"

Using my once threatening bent arm, I gave him a big hug and told him I would be glad to help. As I hugged him, I thought to myself "and we call him slow!"

Ronald Wade Sr.

IT ALL STARTED with a phone call or at least that's when I thought it started. Mid-day, during a class, I was paged over the P.A. system and told that I had a person-to-person call. I had no idea who would be placing such a specialized phone call, but I figured it had to be important, so I quickly assigned my students some independent work and ran to the office. Before I took the phone, the secretary whispered in my ear that it was Mr. Ronald Wade Sr. I was a little confused by that because I knew my student Ronald Wade had a father with the same name but he was in prison in Mississippi. I thought if it was he, maybe he had been released. Well, it was Ronald's father, but he had not been released. He was calling from prison!

I never found out why Mr. Wade was incarcerated, but I did know that he was in a maximum-security prison. At the very beginning of our conversation, I could tell that Mr. Wade was upset, but he was relatively respectful. He quickly made it very clear though that he did not agree or approve of his son being placed in an EMR self-contained classroom.

Ronald, his two siblings, and his grandmother had moved from the referring school before Ronald's paperwork had been completed, so I had to finish it. Ronald was temporarily placed in my program while he was waiting for approval to be placed in a self-contained class. Though I had not recommended him for this placement, it was obvious that was where he would receive the best help. Mr. Wade called me because he thought I was the teacher who referred and approved his son for the self-contained placement.

Ronald was an incredibly sweet boy and had a great sense of humor, but he needed full-time attention. He definitely wouldn't get that attention in a regular classroom of twenty-five or more students with three hours a day in my program. Over the phone, I could hear the father's frustration with his son's situation but unfortunately for Mr. Wade, even though he was the father, the decision-making power was not actually his. It was his mother's. Mrs. Wade was Ronald Jr.'s grandmother and legal guardian, and she had agreed and signed for Ronald Jr.'s self-contained placement in an EMR classroom.

Mrs. Wade was a wonderful woman who was doing a fabulous and difficult job raising three grandchildren, all of whom were having academic and social problems. It was reported that when Ronald Sr. was sent to prison, his wife, Ronald Jr.'s mother, just disappeared. The grandmother was a gentle woman, up in years. Her husband had died a few years earlier, her son was in prison, and her daughter-in-law skipped out on her responsibilities, leaving the three grandchildren in Mrs. Wade's care. Though she had no one to help her, all three children were improving under her watch. It was sad that during every one of our conferences, Mrs. Wade kept apologizing that since she was so old and didn't have much money, she could only offer her grandchildren time and love. I tried to explain to her that those were the most important elements every child needed, but she always felt she fell short.

Throughout all our meetings and phone calls, Mrs. Wade explained that when she received information from me or the school, she would send it on to her son. Evidently, the father never liked and never agreed to this placement for his son. I knew nothing of his dissention until his phone call.

Speaking with Mr. Wade, I was as cordial as possible while I explained each step taken to assure him this placement would benefit his son far more than his present classroom situation. I reminded him that his son was in a third grade class but functioning basically as a kindergartener. I explained that Ronald had a great attitude but even that was starting to weaken. I spoke with as much conviction (pun definitely intended!) as possible but nothing seemed to sink in for Mr. Wade. He never lost his temper, but he made it very clear he would never approve of his son's placement in a self-contained classroom. He claimed it would cause a label to hang over his son's head, and he wouldn't hear of it. (I am not sure if Mr. Wade realized the label he gave his son by being a dad in a maximum-security prison, but I digress.) I told him I understood the concern he had about his son's reputation, and I tried to explain that Ronald already had a label of being slow by the children in his regular classroom, and he was feeling the painful effects of the label.

Nothing I said seemed to matter to Mr. Wade. He just demanded over and over again that his son had to stay where he was. Tiring of this aimless conversation with Mr. Wade, I simply said that Ronald's legal guardian had already signed permission for the change of placement and the other school officials had also given their written approval. The placement was going to happen.

Mr. Wade was furious with me but kept his composure as best he could. He ended our conversation by saying that if his son was placed in an EMR self-contained classroom, he, Mr. Wade, had plenty of friends on the outside who owed him favors, and he would make sure that I paid for ignoring his demands!

I was so young then and in my immortal stage of life that

Mr. Wade's threat didn't faze me, and I didn't take it seriously. Only now, when I am recounting the whole situation, does it unnerve me. I am much older, a bit wiser, and I feel my mortality, so I know I would have reacted very differently if the same situation happened now. At that particular time though, I simply told Mr. Wade that I was sorry he didn't understand the situation and that I wished he could see the placement was in his son's best interest. I added that there was really nothing he could do about changing it since Mrs. Wade was responsible for that decision, and I was sure she would keep him up to date with Ronald's progress. Though I was still talking, Mr. Wade abruptly hung up on me.

It took a total of eight months to get Ronald placed in a self-contained EMR classroom. Not surprisingly, Ronald did very well there. Fortunately for me, none of Mr. Wade's friends ever visited me, so I guess he must have decided that his son was where he was supposed to be after all. I am sure Mrs. Wade kept him well informed of Ronald's progress.

Thank you, Mrs. Wade!

Playground Fight

I NEVER UNDERSTOOD why the school system did this but over the summers my old trailer would be removed and replaced with a *new* old trailer. It didn't make sense, but since I knew there was no benefit to complain about the inconvenience it caused me, I just toted my materials and rug samples to the new classroom at the start of each school year. The trailers may have been old, but I grew to appreciate them.

Though we still shared the trailer with the speech teacher, her side of the trailer was vacant most of the time because Mrs. Taylor was servicing students in several other schools as well as ours due to budget cuts. That meant we had the trailer basically to ourselves. Over my last three years at this school, I learned that working in a trailer allowed my students and me a great deal of flexibility with our noise and our activities since we were not near any other classrooms.

The one continued flaw was that the trailer was always placed right by the playground. To lessen the visual distractions, I covered the lower sections of the trailer windows with construction paper but the noise was a different story. I didn't have to worry too much about the noise in the winter since most of the time we had our windows shut, but during the hot days, when our air conditioner was normally not working, the windows had to be open, which permitted the alluring noise of all the children on the playground to fill our classroom.

One particular day when our windows had to be open, the level of noise was so extreme that it was impossible for even me to ignore. I knew there was a problem because the ruckus was deafening, and it was not the least bit playful sounding. Before I could look out the window to see what was happening, two of my students who were at recess with their regular classroom friends stormed into our room. They were shouting an enthusiastic announcement of a fight on the playground! These two Paul Revere students seemed to be competing with each other to be the honored one to deliver this, in their eyes, awesome and exciting news. What made it even more exciting (to them) was that one of the combatants was a student who attended my class.

That hailed combatant and member of my class was Thad. The fact that he was in a fight didn't surprise me but what did surprise me was *whom* he was fighting. Terence was definitely the wrong person to fight. Both he and Thad were sixth graders but Terence was the tallest boy in the school and was solid muscle. Thad, on the other hand, was well built but was the smallest of the sixth graders. Because of his size, he always seemed to act like he had to prove himself, which caused him to instigate many fights. Terence was quite nice and far from a bully and would more than likely never choose to be in a fight unless he was provoked. Obviously, Thad had done some provoking.

Through my still limited experience, I had learned to keep a low profile emotionally and with my movements while working with my students to help them stay as calm as possible, especially in critical times like this. I slowly got up from my seat and looked out the top of the window and sure enough, there were the two boys duking it out. Seeing the nasty punches being thrown, I could tell it was definitely a serious fight.

Regardless of how calm I stayed, my students seemed instantly possessed with the insatiable need to be outside with the other students. They totally forgot any rules in the class and headed for the door as if they could just leave. I was shocked at how these sweet children quickly turned into such blood-thirsty spectators a person might see at a wrestling mania show! With an extremely irritated voice and facial expression to match, I yelled that under no circumstance were they allowed out of our room, and they were to get back in their seats and stay there. Oh my! They were furious with this unfair restriction and complained that the other students on the playground got to see the fight. Their arguments landed on deaf ears since I couldn't be bothered with their whining. Thankfully, Mrs. Martin was working late that day, so she was there to corral my students, allowing me to deal with Thad, Terence, and the other students outside.

Even though I had been teaching for a little more than two years, I had never witnessed a fight before, let alone been the one responsible to break up one. I had no clue what I was going to do as I ran up to the commotion. For just a few seconds, I stood and watched what was happening. Looking at the whole picture, it was obvious to me what the solution was. I quickly went up to the crowd of cheering students and started shouting at them, declaring that recess was over, and they had to get back to their classes immediately! As I was yelling for them to disperse, I promised two weeks detention to anyone who lingered. I heard many complaints but again, my voice and facial expression seemed to convince them I meant business, and they all reluctantly complied. The whole time I was emptying the playground, I never said a word to Terence or Thad. They were the least of my concerns. I believed that most fights like this one were caused by peer pressure, so I rationalized that if I eliminated the cheering squad, which I believed was their fuel for fighting, the boys would realize there was no reason to throw punches any longer.

I couldn't understand why this fight broke out until I talked later with the teacher who was on playground duty. She had stepped away for just a few minutes to help a student who had been hurt and sure enough that short amount of time was just enough for this skirmish to take on a life of its own. When she saw what was happening, she came running over and helped get the last few stragglers back to class and was mortified at what happened during her brief absence. I had already learned how fast certain kids could take advantage of unsupervised moments, and I assured her it could have happened to any of us. Then, since I knew she needed to get back to her class, I volunteered to take care of the two fighting boys.

After all the other students were off the playground, I stood to the side of the main building where the two boys couldn't see me and watched them because I needed to make sure I was right. And I was. The cheering squad was the fuel for the fight and with them gone, the slugs got fewer and weaker, then finally they stopped.

The boys never said a word to each other, but they communicated with their body language. If scores were being kept, Terence won hands down and Thad respectfully conceded. Terence brushed himself off and started back to the main building while Thad stayed sitting on the ground, facing the woods. It seemed that he needed some private time and since his next class was mine, I left him alone. I knew I could keep my eye on him from the trailer window.

Back in my room, I announced to all my students that no one, and I meant *no one*, was to say a word about the fight to Thad when he came to class. Everyone grumbled but they knew they had better comply. About five minutes after I had returned, Thad sheepishly walked in the room. He was a wreck. I greeted him kindly by saying that I was glad he was here and encouraged him to take some time to go to the bathroom to wash up. I told him not to hurry and when he came back, I would have his work out and ready for him. He gave me a grateful but embarrassed smile and left the room as quietly as he had entered.

Since I believed it was not the fight that was the problem but instead the issue was Thad's continued poor self-image, I never directly talked about the playground fight with him. It wasn't necessary since there was no reason to state the obvious. What happened at the end of the day was quite special though. A few minutes after the dismissal bell rang, I heard someone running up the ramp to my room huffing and puffing. It was Thad. He poked his head in the doorway and blurted out, "Thank you, Miss Chandler!" I wasn't sure what he was thanking me for; it could have been for saving his neck from the fight or maybe for not rubbing his nose in the situation after the fact. It didn't really matter why he was thanking me. I was just thrilled he knew I was on his side.

Darren

THERE WAS A great deal that distracted Darren, a fourth grader, from concentrating on his classwork. It could be a plane overhead, the sound of people walking by, a student near Darren talking about something interesting to him or even a fly tapping on a window pane. Nothing though, distracted him more than having ashy skin. For me, I would describe it as dry skin, but my students affected by this condition insisted that I call it "ashy."

I don't like dry (oops, I mean ashy) skin either, but I had to learn the absolute urgency for some of my students to correct this skin problem as quickly as possible. Knees and elbows tended to be the most frequent offenders. Knees were obvious, but elbows had to be pointed out by other students.

Darren usually came to school well dressed and well-greased. On a handful of occasions, he would come to school without the greased skin. Those were the worst days for both of us.

On one particular day, Stacy, a second grader, pointed out that Darren had ashy elbows. She was definitely the town crier when it came to announcing that someone had ashy skin and though I appreciated her concern for others, her reaction and attention to the skin issue always interfered with our class. To her though, it was important to let Darren know about his condition.

Now that Darren was aware of his ashy elbows, he tugged and pulled at his short sleeve shirt, constantly shrugging his shoulders trying to hide his elbows but to no avail. Since he couldn't cover them up, he tried to fix the problem by using his spit but that made the skin look worse. His groaning and nervous behavior had gone on for over thirty minutes. Though he was definitely disrupting my class, I felt sorry for him and knew I had to help out the poor guy.

Since Stacy loved to be a helper, I asked her to go to the office and ask Mrs. McKay if the school had any skin cream we could use. It turned out that the school didn't have any cream, but Mrs. McKay had some in her purse, and she gave it to Stacy for us to use.

When Stacy walked into the room and handed the cream to Darren, he looked as if he had been given a new lease on life. He quickly spread the cream all over his knees, arms, elbows and face. When he was satisfied with how he looked, I had him return the bottle to Mrs. McKay so he could personally thank her. When he returned, Darren was able to concentrate, and we were able to complete our class time successfully.

After this condition showed up a few more times, I started noticing the difference in my students' behavior when their skin was ashy as opposed to when it was greased. Ashy skin definitely got in the way of my teaching and my students' ability to stay focused. Realizing the importance of greased skin, I went to a drugstore and bought a huge bottle of skin cream. I took it to school and created a mini lesson to share with all the students. During each class, we talked about our skin and ways to care for it. I explained that using cream was one way to help our skin. Each student was allowed to use some of the cream to rub on their knees, elbows, legs, arms, and face. I ended each mini lesson by telling them that many, if not all of them, might need to use cream at one time or another. I continued by saying that if they were not able to use some cream at home or needed more while at school, I would always keep a bottle in the bottom drawer of my desk. I made sure everyone knew it was available to any of them at any time.

For me, it wasn't surprising that no one ever abused the cream privilege. Students of all degrees of skin color used it, though it seemed the darker the skin, the more urgent the need for the skin cream. Many students who were not even scheduled to be with me but needed a good greasing would come in the room quietly, get some cream, and then leave. I never minded, and it never disrupted my classes when students did this. They were just taking care of themselves.

Children are no different than adults needing to be comfortable with their environment and with themselves, yet they are expected to endure discomfort silently. During assemblies, I would note that the children were all made to sit on the hard floor and expected to sit still while their teachers sat on chairs. In classes, I would see teachers with a glass of water or cup of coffee on their desk so they could take a sip whenever they needed to quench their thirst while children were only allowed to take a quick drink of water when they were scheduled. Then the obvious difference I saw was with the availability to the restrooms. In most cases, teachers had the flexibility to use the restroom whenever they needed. Yet children were told to "hold it" until the allotted time. I am not trying to criticize teachers. On the contrary, I agree that they should take care of themselves. What we need to do is allow our students to take care of themselves also. Yes, there are a few students who might take advantage of this freedom, but let's start rewarding the good kids with the right to monitor their own physical condition.

Darren confirmed the importance of this one afternoon. He had just finished greasing himself, and I asked if he was ready to get to work. He simply replied, "Yep, *now* I'm ready *to think!*"

Stacy's Math

STACY, MY STUDENT who made sure her peers were well greased, entered my program when she was in first grade. She was tiny and frail looking but looks can definitely be deceiving. She was actually one tough cookie! No one, and I mean no one, was ever going to mess with her or do her wrong. Stacy may have had troubles with academics, but she was definitely street smart. This little girl had the energy supply of a ballet troupe packed in her petite body because it seemed that her body always had to be in motion. If she wasn't literally dancing or jumping up and down, rest assured some part of her body was in motion.

There was no medical reason for Stacy to look the way she did, and I am certain she is quite pretty now, but back then, she had such an old looking face. Her head could have been put on an eighty-year-old body and it would have fit better than on her tiny six-year-old body. Stacy's one physical saving grace was that she had the most captivating and powerful smile, and the nice thing about it was that she used it all the time.

Across the academic board, Stacy had difficulty committing information to memory. She would eventually develop reading skills after being taught over a few days or maybe a week of many and varied drills. Math, though, was an entirely different problem for her. Nothing seemed to click or stick. Stacy would try and try, but the next day or even the next ten minutes after a new skill had been introduced, she could neither recall it nor process it properly. There were so many days of emotional pain for her, but she had such a desire to learn, and she was committed to completing her assignments. This math glitch Stacy had was so confusing to me. I tried every way I could to help her understand the skills. I realized that if I was confused and frustrated, I was sure Stacy had to be totally bewildered. She would break down so many days in class and cry out that she knew how to do the problem but at that moment, she couldn't remember how! On those occasions, I would just hold her as she cried. We would talk a bit off the subject, and when she had regained her composure, we would get back to the work at hand. I hated to see Stacy suffer. She wanted to learn and her effort was there, so I was determined to find a solution for her.

Since Stacy had to move her body and desperation had set in for me, I created a *new* method using Stacy's body. I traced her tiny footprints, made many copies, cut them out, put numbers on each one and then laminated them. I needed her to understand *how* the math worked. Using her whole body was the only method I could think of to help her and amazingly it worked!

It worked at least when she had to compute addition and subtraction problems. We started with numbers from zero to ten. In preparation of doing her work, Stacy would lay her "feet" down on the floor with the numbers in the right order. For addition, she would stand on zero and wait to be shown her math problem to compute. I would write a problem on the board: for example: 5 + 4 =. Standing on zero, she would walk up five then walk up four and then lift her last foot up and magically, there was the correct answer! It was a thrill to see how excited she got *walking through* her math problems. We ended up with well over a hundred of Stacy's little footprints all over the trailer by the time she progressed into higher addition and subtraction.

This *total body* method worked for Stacy. No one minded that her tracks were everywhere. After she developed her skills and no longer needed them, her tiny prints made great wall decorations.

I don't agree with the use of calculators in elementary math classes because I believe students need to know *and understand* how the actual math concept works. I also believe it is a great mental exercise. Achieving the correct answer is absolutely essential in math but understanding the process and concept is also important. In Stacy's situation though, I was totally in favor of letting her use a calculator. The problem I ran into was that calculators were not allowed in her regular classroom. Without the use of a calculator, I knew that Stacy wouldn't be able to compute her problems without at least the use of her fingers. Yes, I believe in the use of fingers computing math problems! It is tactile and some children are tactile learners. I had a marvelous math professor in college who adamantly supported the use of fingers when teaching math. He felt it should not only be allowed but even encouraged, and he made his point very well by holding up his hands in class one day. One hand showed a thumb and four fingers and the other hand, deformed, showed a thumb and one finger. He said he was blessed with seven digits and was grateful to be able to use them and if anyone was lucky enough to have a complete set, "then by God's grace, use them!"

Stacy was one of the lucky ones with a complete set, and she used her fingers to do many of her calculations in my class. Unfortunately, her classroom teacher was from the old school mentality and forbid the use of finger counting. This teacher believed it was cheating so she would purposely embarrass any student in front of the entire class if she caught them using their fingers. In my opinion, this is an example of misplaced priorities by the teacher. What is more important: a student's dignity and knowledge of a math skill or humiliating a student and missing a chance to reach a child? It seems pretty obvious to me, but it is not for so many teachers (and parents).

It only took two years for Stacy to develop her ability to compute double digit addition and subtraction problems (without regrouping). Life with Stacy was going fairly well. Then third grade came and with it came multiplication. This concept was either going to make or break Stacy. For a while I thought it was going to break her. The puzzling situation was that she understood how it all worked but to commit the math problems to memory was just not happening.

After two months of misery trying to learn multiple factors, I decided to concentrate on one number sentence: 3 x 7 = 21. For the next two and a half weeks, this was the only problem we practiced. I would sneak in her regular classroom and pop the question: "What is 3 x 7?" I might find her in the cafeteria, on the school bus, or in the restroom and pop the question. Her classmates in my room, as well as in her regular classroom, caught on to what I was doing, and they would act as lookouts and warn Stacy that I was coming. I didn't really care if she looked up the answer or if someone told her. It was a fun game, and I knew over time, she would get the answer on her own.

When the fateful moment happened, I was thrilled that she was in my room. All I can remember about that session was that she and I were doing a reading assignment when out of the blue, I popped the question. Without hesitation, Stacy blurted out "21." There was a split second that it didn't register with Stacy, the other students, or me what she had just done. Then the sudden realization of what she had accomplished swept across her tiny, *old*, precious face. This little person started dancing all around the room hooting and hollering. She even jumped up onto the round table and started to do a funky dance singing out her new-found number sentence with the correct answer at the end!

While I was applauding and congratulating Stacy, I was surprised by what else I witnessed happening around the room. All of my other students who had endured listening to the torturous drills that Stacy suffered through were cheering with excitement, applauding, and hugging her with genuine support for her and her accomplishments. That all too common lump in my throat returned, and I quietly grabbed a tissue to dry my cheeks.

Math continued to be difficult for Stacy, but she did start retaining her factors and learned to retrieve the answers with minimal effort. Until that glorious day though, I never realized just how much my other students had been emotionally involved with Stacy's plight through the months and years she struggled with her math. At that moment, I recognized that her success was a triumphant time for us all!

Stacy's Rendition

AS I EXPLAINED in the previous story, Stacy was a precious and hardworking student. In my opinion, she was perfect with the exception of two major idiosyncrasies: she couldn't sit still and she couldn't stop talking. Usually, she did both simultaneously. I am sure it is an exaggeration but it seemed like some body-part on Stacy was always moving. Her movements weren't subtle either. For example, while she was sitting, Stacy would swing her legs so hard under her chair that it would cause her whole body to bounce up and down. She would be bouncing like this while talking, and for me, it was very distracting. Another example would be that she couldn't sit and talk. She would walk nervously around the room in a figure eight, zigzag, or circling formation.

Whatever method she chose, it was accompanied by an upbeat and excited monologue. If she happened to stay in one place, her mouth and hands seemed to move in double time. I used to tease her by saying she was my human-sized jumping bean. I even noticed this behavior when she had to stand in line with her regular class. While in line, the students weren't allowed to talk so she would bend and straighten her knees and bounce up and down shaking her hands in front of her. She just couldn't be still.

Stacy's nervous and seemingly endless movement drove me insane but making her be still wasn't a priority. My focus was to help her learn the required math and reading skills, but I must admit her jittery behavior was an exhausting struggle to ignore on many days. I knew that dealing with her energy would become a focus of ours eventually. I just didn't expect it to happen so abruptly.

One morning at school, Mrs. Douglas, the North Carolina State contracted psychologist, had come in to do some evaluations and re-evaluations of some special education students in our school. Several of the students scheduled for testing were in my program, and I needed to talk with her prior to working with these students. I had a great deal to do before class started, however, when I ran into Mrs. Douglas at the main office, I walked with her to the room where she would be testing, and we discussed my students on her list. I had worked with Mrs. Douglas on many occasions before and was pleased she would be doing the testing because she worked well with the students, and I respected her detailed analysis of the test results. I realized it was almost time for my first class to start so we wrapped up our conversation, and I quickly headed to my room.

Stacy was one of my students who came first thing in the morning. I usually started working with her as soon as she walked in the room just to get her on track, then she could complete her independent work. Though my pre-class activities that morning were a bit hectic, I thought I was in a patient and cheerful mood, but apparently I was not. Stacy was moving, bouncing, and chattering as usual. I am not sure why, but I hit my limit of bounces and erratic movements, and it was only eight thirty in the morning! I just couldn't take it anymore.

I playfully took Stacy by the arms and gently placed her in a chair. Smiling, I told her to sit still just for a moment and watch me. I then proceeded to imitate her with all her cute and fun but also annoying antics. Stacy's *still position* didn't last long when she caught on to what I was doing. She started hopping up and down yelling for me to stop. She even came over and yanked my arm demanding for me to quit it. I could tell she was okay with what I was doing because she and the other students were having a good healthy belly laugh as they watched me. In between laughing and yelling at me to stop, she said I was making her nervous and that she couldn't hear everything I was saying and it wasn't funny anymore. And yet she kept laughing!

While I continued the *Stacy Rendition*, I started explaining why I was mimicking her. I wanted her to see *and* experience what people around her had to deal with in regard to her behavior. I explained that I absolutely loved her, and I loved her energy and enthusiasm, but she needed to taper her jumpiness down a bit for my sake, if for no other reason.

I saw that I had her attention so I really turned on the dramatics. The other students were howling at this point, and I realized they too were affected by Stacy's over-the-top hyper behavior. In my excitement, I jumped on the table and started dancing and spinning around, just as Stacy would do when she was about to pop out of her skin with energy.

I think it took me a while to notice that the children's laughter seemed to change direction and intensity. Through the commotion, I could hear gentle giggles from Stacy. That was strange. I knew something was wrong, so I turned around to the front of the room. There in the doorway was the psychologist! She was standing there looking right at me (who knows for how long) with the most puzzled face. Mrs. Douglas smiled and said that she obviously caught me at a bad time so she asked if she could meet with me at a more convenient time. I simply replied, "That would be great." What else could I say? As soon as the door shut behind her, the laughter welled up again, but this time it wasn't toward Stacy but toward me. I had to join in the laughter.

Unfortunately, I was not able to talk with Mrs. Douglas that day but she left a note in my box with the names of the students she still needed to test. I read through the list and as I came to the last name, I had to chuckle. There on the last line was the name, *Kathy Chandler: immediate testing necessary!* She ended it with a smiley face. I am glad she had a good sense of humor or at least I hoped she was kidding!

A Visitor

IT WAS A cold rainy day, one of those great days to curl up on a couch, read a book, and take a nap. At least that was what I thought to myself, as I sat in my trailer working with a few of my students. I couldn't really complain though because moods were calm and everyone was quietly working on independent assignments. The only thing different this day was that Mrs. Martin and I had to talk above the rain tapping at the windows and pounding on the trailer's metal roof.

Our serene morning abruptly ended when Jake and Tanner, fourth grade boys of mine, burst in through the trailer doors, causing the glass door to slam against the wall. They ran toward me yelling and shouting something, but I couldn't make any sense of what they were saying. I wasn't worried because their faces were ear-to-ear smiles though I was curious to find out what type of mischief they were conjuring up this time.

As they were coming toward me, I saw Tanner was holding his light-weight, black jacket, but it was all wadded up and soaking wet. Jake got to me first and put his face inches from mine yelling so loud I still couldn't understand what he was saying. While he was slapping his hands on the table with great enthusiasm, Tanner was yelling at him to be quiet. Tanner took the words right out of my mouth, but I meant it for both of them!

When challenging situations presented themselves with my students, I had learned to gather as much information as I could before I got involved. With these two though, it was imperative that I heard all the information before I got entangled in whatever web of mischief they were spinning since they were continually getting into trouble! Unfortunately, at that moment, I knew nothing.

No sooner did Tanner quiet Jake down than he started yelling the same garbled words to me. The only emphasized word I could hear was that they found "it," whatever "it" was. Finally, Tanner plopped the wet, wadded-up jacket on my table. Though he was trying to protect the scrunched-up jacket with his hands, he still managed to jump up and down with Jake.

Using a very controlled and soft tone, I asked them to quiet down and tell me what was in Tanner's jacket. With that innocent request, the boys burst out with laughter again and began jumping up and down with even more enthusiasm. Admittedly, I was struggling with my own desire to yell at them to be quiet, but I knew I had to stay extremely calm since I had learned (the hard way during previous confrontations with them) that whatever my level of emotion was, they always went much higher!

Tanner managed to stop jumping long enough to slowly reveal the contents of the jacket. As he lifted a portion of the jacket, Tanner's already very large eyes seemed to get even bigger as he stared at the wadded mass. To my surprise and everyone else's (except for Tanner and Jake who were ready to pop with excitement), there was a small, white kitten inside the jacket!

Needless to say, the poor thing was terrified and was clinging onto Tanner's coat for dear life. Its blue eyes were wild and its white fur wet and matted. I reached to pick up the kitten but Tanner gave my hands a quick shove, demanding that I was not to hurt or scare it! Remembering the way the boys entered the trailer with the balled-up jacket, I had to chuckle, but I knew Tanner had no idea how frightened the kitten was because of their actions. I was sure that in Tanner's mind, he and Jake were doing a wonderful job saving the kitten from the nasty weather, and their excitement wasn't harmful. The kitten may have begged to differ, but my initial view of her (as she turned out to be) was that she was physically fine, just terrified!

During the commotion caused by Jake and Tanner, the rest of my class had fallen apart. Everyone was out of his or her seat searching for a good spot to see whatever was to be seen. Many of them were shouting out for their turn to pet the kitten, touch the kitten, or hold the kitten. There was no hope of getting back on track with academics, at least for the time being, and I couldn't very well scold the students to calm down and get back to work when I was just as excited to get my turn to hold the little fur ball!

Calming down a bit, Tanner gently picked up the kitten and cradled her in the palms of his hands. He held her close to his chest and used two fingers to rub her neck all the while whispering soothing words in her ear. Bless the kitten's heart, she became quite peaceful and actually started rubbing against Tanner's fingers. The kitten had forgotten her entrance and settled right into Tanner's now protective hands with no intention of budging. That was until she saw the other children in the room also ready and willing to pet her.

I knew the kitten belonged to someone, but at that moment, the kitten belonged to Jake and Tanner. I put them in charge of dealing with the kitten until I could get a grip on what I should do with this new member of my class.

While I was thinking, Jake and Tanner, along with my other students, solved the immediate problem of who got to hold the kitten. After discussing the situation with each other, they slowly returned to their seats and got back to work. Their solution was that each of the students would have five minutes to hold the kitten, and they drew numbers to determine the turns. Well, at least that was their intended solution. Actually, the kitten took turns with the students on her terms. She would lie on one student's desk for a while, then jump down, walk around, and then hop up on someone else's lap or desk for a while. She was absolutely precious as she worked her way through the room. It seemed the kitten had made herself at home as quickly as she had entered our room. I realized my immediate problem was solved and felt I should also resume my duties in the class, so for the next hour, everyone enjoyed the new member of our room and all was calm.

When the time neared for class to change, I talked to Jake and Tanner about the importance of finding the kitten's real owner. That was not a popular topic. Tanner disagreed firmly and announced that the kitten was his now. He had found her, and he would give her a good home. I tried to rationalize with him, putting him in the place of the boy who may have lost the kitten and was missing her terribly. Tanner couldn't have cared less about that. His only reply was that the boy should have taken better care of the kitten! I tried a few other angles to convince him to search for its owner, but none worked. Finally, out of desperation, I fabricated a school rule saying that animals were not allowed in the school. With a serious tone, I explained that I could get fired if the principal ever found out I had allowed a cat in my class. I said it with such persuasion that Jake and Tanner believed me. They had so much compassion for me that they promised they would never get me fired, but they weren't going to get rid of the cat! I couldn't win, so I decided to surrender my efforts temporarily until I could think of another solution.

While I was trying to conjure up a new reason to get rid of the cat, there was commotion at the front door. What now? Ian, one of my third graders, ran into the room broadcasting that the principal was coming straight to our room. What a clever kid he was; he was trying to help me out and get the boys to get rid of the cat. To my surprise and horror, the principal was really coming, and he was walking up my trailer steps! I couldn't believe it. This man never came to my room. Never! Why did he have to come this particular day, walking all the way to my trailer? And in the rain no less! Why couldn't he have waited, as he always did, and talked with me when he saw me in the office or in the hallways?

Of all days for him to visit my room! I was going to get caught in my lie because there was no rule that I couldn't have an animal in my room. I was a teacher! Of course, I could have animals and as much as I didn't care for this principal, he did have a soft spot in his heart for animals. He wouldn't have minded the cat at all. Though he might not have liked me, he never would have fired me over having a cat in my room.

I had to do something and I had to do it quickly. I jumped up and ran through the foyer area to meet the principal outside so I could let him in on what was happening with the cat. I had just gotten outside the door when there was yet another commotion, but this time it was in the classroom area! The noise and laughter was so loud that I spun around and headed back to the class with the principal right at my heels. Now I might be in trouble! I couldn't even guess what the students had done and just my luck, the principal was right there to witness it all. Sadly, during his reign as principal, I always felt that he was anxious to catch me doing something wrong. Now was his big chance!

In the seconds it took me to turn around and run back through the trailer foyer and into the classroom, all was silent. Everyone was doing his or her own work looking very normal. Something wasn't right. All looked right, but I knew something was going on because things looked too perfect. Even Mrs. Martin was calmly sitting with her students and working as she always did. I was stumbling with my words to the principal because I was trying to make heads or tails out of what had just happened. As I was trying to say something intelligent, I realized what was wrong. I was missing two kids and a cat! My room was far too small for anyone to hide let alone two hyper boys and a cat. So, where were they? I had no idea!

All I knew was that I needed to get rid of the principal without really losing my job. I calmly told him that all was well in the class and asked how I could help him. He had a form for me to fill out and needed it by lunch. I hurriedly promised to get it back to him and thanked him for personally delivering it and walked him out the door.

After he left the room and was out of sight, laughter erupted inside the trailer. I stood there with my hands on my hips and demanded to know where Jake and Tanner were. Everyone, including Mrs. Martin, pointed over my book-shelves. The bookshelves were wonderful to divide the two rooms and give visual privacy but there was an open space of about eighteen inches from the top of the cases to the ceil-ing. Impossible I thought. The boys and the cat couldn't have fit through that small space. That was what I thought until I heard Mrs. Taylor, the speech teacher, call out from the other side of the bookshelves confirming that the boys and the cat had in fact come over the bookshelves, but now they were gone, having left through the trailer's back door. Now I really could get fired! I had lost two students! My fabricated story, or rather my out-and-out lie, made the situation with the kitten even worse.

Mrs. Martin continued class while I ran outside to find the runaways. I didn't have to look far. They were headed back to my room having hidden under the trailer until the principal was out of sight. All Tanner said, as he brushed past me head-ing toward the classroom, was "I told you I wouldn't get you fired!" In the back of my mind, I was thinking at least not yet. One thing I did know was the kitten had to go before things really got out of hand (as if they hadn't already)!

The welcoming committee inside the trailer was waiting with bated breath to see their comrades and mascot return. There was no hope for trying to return to planned activities, so I quickly decided to make the rest of the day one of moral and ethical considerations. In short, what was the right thing to do with the cat? I was out numbered, but I was determined to have the students see my way. I was just as stubborn as they were.

It was lunchtime for everyone, so I thought I would have a few moments to collect my thoughts. Wrong! Jake and Tanner conned their way out of lunch in the cafeteria by telling their teacher I needed to see them. It didn't matter how many times I told some classroom teachers not to send students to my room outside of their regular time without a note from me. It seemed that these less-dedicated teachers were always more than happy to let my students just come to my class any time the students or teachers wanted. In this case, the boys wanted to bring food for the kitten, and they were masters at spinning a tale for the teacher to let them do what they wanted. I did let the boys give the cat some food, but then I marched them back to the cafeteria and asked their classroom teacher not to allow them back to my room until their scheduled time later in the afternoon. On my way back to my classroom, I swung by the office to drop off the completed form that the principal had requested. I certainly didn't want to give him any reason to come back to my room until the kitten was gone!

I know other teachers wouldn't have felt there was a problem because they would simply say that the cat had to go. End of the situation. For me though, I wanted the children to solve their own problem properly without me barreling in and doing it for them. Plus, rarely did Jake and Tanner ever show this much enthusiasm about anything, so I didn't want to squelch their enthusiasm. I realized I had to help them solve their problem with the kitten though, and I knew I had to work quickly.

Jake and Tanner were to return to my room the last hour

of the day. They bolted into the classroom to see if the cat was still there and still okay. They were quickly shushed by a few students because at that moment the kitten was sound asleep on Colton's desk, belly up. Colton and the cat were in such a blissful state, I made both of the returning boys wait their turns to have the cat. Fortunately, the kitten slept a while so I had some time to talk with the boys. I wanted Jake and Tanner to realize they couldn't just keep a kitten. I used the argument that their moms wouldn't allow a strange cat to just be brought home. Tanner gave a whispered scream and said he'd already called his mom, and she agreed that if the cat wasn't claimed, Tanner could bring her home. Big help she was!

I was running out of ideas rapidly. For the remaining activities of the day, I had the boys make *lost and found* posters: one to be put in the office and three to be put along the entrance to the neighborhood next to the school. That got me through the hour. Before they left for home, the boys delivered their posters to the assigned areas and then came back to bid their kitten good night. I repeatedly thanked the boys for doing such a great job on the posters and explained that I was going to leave the kitten inside the trailer in a box with some food. They didn't like the idea, but since they couldn't take the kitten home on the bus that afternoon, they agreed with this plan.

My dilemma was solved but only by default. The owner came to the school the next morning and claimed the kitten. It was painfully sad when Tanner came to class so anxious to see *his* kitten and I had to tell him that the owner had come to claim his kitten and had taken her home. Tanner's world was shaken because he and his mom had bought a collar, kitten food, and other supplies since they thought the kitten was going to be theirs. Now the kitten was gone and Tanner was mournfully quiet. I made sure to tell the boys that the owner was grateful for them taking such good care of his kitten, but the words just fell flat on the boys' ears and hearts. I knew the situation had worked itself out the correct way, but I couldn't help but hurt for both of the boys. It may seem heartless because though I loved the kitten too, I was so glad she was gone.

The day after the kitten had visited was rather dull, and everyone seemed quite somber and lethargic. These low energy days were rare, and I knew it wouldn't be long before we'd have another exciting event occur in our room, so I decided just to enjoy the temporary peace and quiet.

The Ring Mistress

One teacher, one helper, eight kids and a cat!
That's better than any circus act.
Now eight is really twenty-four
But there are really never, never more
(or so I've been told) than eight in the trailer at a time.
Unless you count the cat, and that makes nine.
The kids are all ages between eight and eleven.
And the day the cat came, they were all in heaven-
Up there doing a high wire act
With the cat as the principal acrobat
Cooperating with every zany ploy
Conjured up by each and every girl and boy-
From a cannon ball flying to a tamed lion lying-
'Til the closing bell.
Well, the cat was claimed, the act over, I hope,
But tomorrow the ring mistress will have to cope
With a new act to follow.

Written by Lois Martin

Knowing Something Different

BECAUSE OF THEIR educational challenges, my students seemed as if they were always trying to catch up with their classmates in their regular classroom. They yearned to participate with their friends on the same level in some area, and it was an ongoing struggle. Though it didn't seem right, it was the rut we were in. That is until Mya, now a fifth grader, gave me a great idea.

Mya, Morgan, and Toni came in my room all upset about an easy assignment they had been given in their regular class because the teacher didn't think they could do the class assignment. The teacher was probably right, but it didn't help the girls' feelings at the time. Mya was the loudest to complain. She finally ended her rant with the fact that she wished she knew something the other kids in her class didn't already know. CLICK! A realization came to me as soon as she said that. My students were always trying to follow. They needed to learn how to lead and, as Mya said, know something the other students didn't. I had fallen in the catch-up game, and Mya broke that restricting mindset for me.

I considered the situation for a short while and then

came up with a great idea. I didn't choose it because I knew it would be so successful. Instead, I chose it because it was the only thing I knew that I could teach my students immediately. I also believed that most of their classmates wouldn't know it, and that the girls would enjoy sharing it.

Before telling them what I was considering, I had to make sure they were truly interested. I asked Mya if she really meant what she said. She looked at me quite confused and asked, "Meant what?" I repeated her statement about wanting to know something that her classmates in the other class didn't know. She confirmed that she did, but the tone in her voice revealed the state of defeat that she had accepted.

With a cheerleader's voice, I told Mya and the other two girls that if they were serious, I had something I could teach them, but it would be extra and they would have to work hard to study it. I explained that people only knew extra information when they took the initiative to learn on their own and asked if they were up to the challenge to learn something most of their classmates wouldn't know. Overhearing my conversation, I had *expectantly* attracted the interest of my other students in the class as well as the three girls. I repeated my question to everyone now. Mya excitedly interrupted me, demanding to know what in the world I was talking about.

Getting the rest of the class' attention, I told them to watch me. In sign language I said, "My name is Miss Chandler." While I was doing the signing, the students were confused and kept asking what I was doing. Toni got so irritated at me she even grabbed my right arm to make me stop. When I finished signing my sentence, I explained that I was *talking* in sign language. Even though they didn't quite understand, my students, especially my girls, were thrilled at the thought of learning it and asked me how I knew sign language.

I told the story of when I was in college and my roommate had to take a sign language course. I didn't have anything to do on the night that her class met, and I thought it would be fun, so I decided to take the class with her. Never in a million years did I ever expect to use the skills I learned in that class, let alone years later teach the basics of sign language.

My students knew that I had been a lifeguard in college but that was all. This time around, I elaborated a bit more. What they hadn't been told was that only six months after the sign-language class was over, a deaf-mute student at the university started coming to the pool. Though I didn't know detailed signing, what I did know helped me communicate a bit more with this student than if I hadn't known the language at all. I continued expounding on the fact that here I was, many years after I had taken the class, getting ready to teach my students the alphabet and some basic signs. I couldn't miss the opportunity to point out that learning extra information, information that at the time might seem frivolous and unnecessary, was always exciting because they would never know when that information might be able to help them.

I had caught everyone's attention so I quickly switched plans for the day. My well-organized lesson plan for that day, like many days, took a definite turn, and sign language was now our focus. After the first day, I didn't make anyone participate if they didn't want to but for that day, we all needed to give it a try. By just introducing the first five letters of the alphabet, we had many words we could practice signing. And did we practice! Everyone seemed to be fascinated with the new mode of communication, so there was a great deal of excitement, energy, and laughter.

The next day, those who didn't want to continue learning the signs were allowed to return to their previously assigned work. We never spent much time in class practicing the signs and alphabet; that was to be done on the student's personal time outside of class. Over a few days and weeks, some students dropped by the wayside and others practiced a little and learned a little. Then there were the hardy few who really wanted to learn the signs and the alphabet. It was so satisfying to watch them use and enjoy their new-found skill.

The true success from teaching my students basic sign language was with my three girls. They had a wonderful time showing off their sign language skills to their friends in the regular classroom. Sometimes I would even find them at recess practicing spelling words from class with their friends!

For me, it was an incredibly helpful teaching tool to be able to spell words in sign language to many of my students. For example, prior to learning the alphabet for sign language, if I was working with one student and another needed help with a word, that child had to wait until I was finished with the other student. Now, with many of them, I could just sign the spelling of the word or a basic answer to their question and everyone stayed working. It was wonderful! Along with learning the alphabet, I taught them some very basic conversational signs that we also had fun using from time to time.

Early one afternoon, I found that I had to go into Mya, Morgan, and Toni's regular classroom to deliver some paperwork to their teacher. When I walked into the room, the girls saw me and loudly whispered my name and waved. As I started to raise my hand to wave back, their teacher yelled at them to be quiet. I quietly lowered my hand but smiled so they knew I saw them.

Their teacher and I talked briefly and after she thanked me, I turned around to leave. Maybe it was the kid in me, but I had to look back over my shoulder toward my girls to at least smile a *good-bye* to them. I'm so glad I did. They were all watching me and I was met with three beautiful smiling faces. Just as I was ready to turn away, Mya raised her hand to show me a sign. It's amazing how powerful three small words can be even when said with a fist showing only three fingers. I had to return the same sign because I wanted her to know that I loved her too.

Earphones

ONE AFTERNOON JAKE, Tanner, Richard, Mya, Morgan, Toni, and I were having an exhilarating and extremely entertaining discussion. Everyone was participating and having a wonderful time. While we were talking, I heard the back door of my trailer open and someone enter. I knew it wasn't a student because they all knew to come in the front door. With that said, it had to be a teacher. The ones who came in the back door or who didn't knock before they entered my room were usually teachers I didn't particularly care for. The teachers who respected my class and me would heed the very large sign that was placed on the back door, which in bold letters read "Please Use the Front Door. Do Not Enter Here. Thank You!"

Despite the students pointing behind me and whispering the name "Mrs. Davis," I kept talking. I cringed when I heard who it was, because she was one of my least favorite people in the whole school. I don't think she heard me and it probably wouldn't have made a difference if she had, but with a sarcastic edge, I loudly claimed, "No one would be so rude and thoughtless to enter our room through the back door."

Trying my best to ignore the approaching steps of the

rude intruder, I kept talking. Incredibly, this woman walked from behind me right into our circle, interrupting my conversation. Placing herself directly in front of me, Mrs. Davis belted out, as if I were invisible, that she needed to see Mya, Morgan, and Toni immediately! I was so shocked by her behavior that it took me a moment to react to what I was witnessing. This woman had the gall to then start yelling at all three of my girls, accusing them of stealing earphones from the library and demanding that they return the devices immediately or she would call the police! She continued by describing them as simple thieves!

Mrs. Davis began spewing out more accusations toward my girls, but I finally got my wits about me and forcefully stood in between my girls and her. Somewhat controlled, I declared that I would not tolerate her barging into my room, disrupting my class, and accusing my students without discussing the problem with me first. I directed her to leave immediately and added that she had better leave through the front door.

By this time, Jake and Tanner were quietly teasing the girls. They were crying and moaning, claiming that they hadn't taken any earphones while Richard was just watching the drama unfold. Mrs. Davis stood there and started to say something else to the girls, but I quickly interrupted her again. This time I vehemently demanded that she leave, stating that she had done enough damage. As she passed the girls, she pointed to them threatening and said, "I will get you!" In disbelief of her arrogance, I shouted, "Leave!" She instantly glared at me growling that I had better do something with those thieves as she darted evil eyes toward the girls and grumbled under her breath that they were nothing but trouble. With that, I yelled even louder, "Get out of my room, NOW!" pointing to the door, which she proceeded to stomp through and slam.

When she was gone, total chaos erupted. The girls began sobbing; Jake and Tanner were misbehaving as they took advantage of the moment, and Richard was warning me that the next group of students was on its way.

Because Richard had proven himself time and time again to be able to think on his feet in chaotic times like this, I asked him to go outside and hold my next group from entering the classroom and keep them on the porch. Thankfully, he rushed out to take care of that particular problem. As for me, I had several things to take care of. First, I had to squelch all of Jake and Tanner's shenanigans. That was rather easy because I just promised them that if they didn't get quiet immediately, get back in their seats and get to work, they would be sent to the office to see the principal. Thankfully, he was one person they didn't want to see if they were in trouble. Finally, I had to deal with the girls. My patience for whining and sobbing was almost nonexistent at any time let alone when there was so much confusion. Trying to mask my frustration with Mrs. Davis as well as with them, I curtly encouraged them to stop crying and sit down so we could talk. They sat down, but they kept sobbing. I desperately needed silence, and since I seemed to be on a roll for yelling, I shouted at them to get quiet immediately. There was sudden silence. With a fake but kinder voice, I reassured them that I believed they hadn't taken the earphones, but they had to stop crying.

After Richard came back in the room, Jake, Tanner, and he were talking. Despite the intensity of my discussion with the girls, I couldn't help overhear some of what the boys were discussing. What I heard piqued my interest, so I excused myself from the girls and went over to where the boys were sitting and asked if there was a problem. Little did I know the can of worms I would open by asking such a simple question.

Without hesitation, Richard confronted me boldly stating that he believed I was rude to Mrs. Davis by yelling at her to leave the trailer. He reminded me that I had told them over and over to never lower themselves to the inappropriate behavior of someone else. With a slight hesitation in his voice,

Richard looked right at me and claimed that I looked just like Mrs. Davis when I was yelling!

I was crushed with his words and his observation, but I knew he was right. The other boys started laughing at me but Richard was silent, just staring at me with such a disillusioned look. I could tell he was confused with my mixed messages but mostly, I could tell he was disappointed in me. That was the hardest part to swallow. I had disappointed my sweet, sweet Richard!

I held my composure and confessed that he was right, and I was sorry for behaving so poorly. Though I could explain my actions, it still didn't excuse my behavior. I added that he did the right thing to point out my mistake, making me aware of what I had done. Promising not to repeat my poor behavior, I assured Richard that I would do whatever I could to correct the situation. In my head, I knew that meant I would have to *eat crow*, and the very thought of that made me wince, but none of that mattered. What mattered was that I had disappointed Richard, and I had to make that right.

Being an inquisitive person, Richard asked how the situation could possibly be rectified. With all the students listening, I explained that I would need to go to Mrs. Davis, apologize for yelling, and then ask when she was free to discuss her concerns with my girls. Nodding, Richard smiled and agreed that was a good idea. He asked if that was going to be hard for me to do. I admitted that apologizing was definitely not going to be easy. Unfortunately, Richard asked the innocent and simple question, "Why?" I knew what I was about to say was not going to be easy to explain, but I needed to be honest. With a deep breath, I confessed that apologizing to Mrs. Davis would be hard because I didn't like her. The kids' immediate reaction to this admission let me know I was in for a long discussion.

The looks and gasps of disbelief written on their faces were almost comical. A teacher didn't like another teacher?

How could that be? I attempted to explain that no matter what my personal feelings were for Mrs. Davis, it gave me no right to treat her the way I had. Jake never missed voicing the obvious and, using the mannerisms of a court jester, he revealed that it was obvious Mrs. Davis didn't like me either. Thankfully, hearing his humorous yet accurate observation, we all had a good laugh that lightened the heavy atmosphere. Though Jake may have been right, I admitted that no matter how she acted, I should never have lowered myself as I had because I didn't want to mirror someone I didn't like.

Seeing our class time fly by, I assured all of them that we would discuss this issue further, but I wanted them to be kind and respectful to Mrs. Davis no matter what my feelings were toward her. Mrs. Davis was their librarian, and she worked very hard to get the library in excellent condition for all the students. That was the truth.

Tanner piped up and stated that he liked Mrs. Davis but questioned how he could like her if I didn't like her. The sincerity and innocence of his question just melted my heart. I gave him a side hug and supported the fact that he liked Mrs. Davis. Still holding onto him, I asked if he liked me. Shocked by my question, he immediately replied, "Certainly! ... Duh!" With this definitive answer, I inquired if he could still like me and be respectful to me even though Mrs. Davis, someone else he admired, didn't like me. He quickly countered, "Certainly!" and followed with an even louder "DUH!" Feeling a bit like I was giving a courtroom summation, I wrapped up our conversation by saying that he and the others should continue liking and respecting Mrs. Davis, regardless of how she and I felt about one another.

My head was throbbing, time was still flitting by, and I had a handful of impatient students waiting outside. The frustrating part was that I hadn't scratched the surface with the girls' situation. They were going to have to wait a little while longer so I could get my next class in the room and busy working on their lessons. Genuinely apologizing for the continued delay, I explained to the girls that I had to work with the students who just came in so they could get started on their assignments. The girls grumbled and rolled their eyes making sure I was aware that they were annoyed, but they knew there was nothing else to do but wait.

In came the students who had been waiting outside and since they had no explanation for why they had been stuck outside for so long, they were wired. Now I had to calm them down! My patience was gone. I could hear the tone in my voice get harsher and shorter. As I was losing my patience, I heard Miss Watkin's words of wisdom ringing in my head. She said that the minute a teacher yelled, she or he instantly lost control of the situation. Well, I was on the verge of yelling at innocent children. Because I didn't want to lose control, I had to make some quick adjustments.

When all the students were in their seats, I confessed to them that I was having a challenging afternoon and asked for everyone's help. I explained that I was in the middle of a very difficult situation that needed to be dealt with immediately and admitted I was confused, upset, and needed some quiet time to get my thoughts back on track. Though I couldn't elaborate on the details, I was ready to lose my temper and asked for their understanding and help. No sooner had I finished talking, all of these precious students sat right down and quickly got quiet.

Taking advantage of the temporary sane moment, these students and I began working on their lessons. This mini reprieve gave me a break from my shredded emotions and calmed me down. After a half hour, I had all the children working on their independent assignments, thanked them for helping me, and then excused myself to go talk with the three girls, who also had benefitted from the short break.

When I sat down with the girls, they were in a more controlled state although they still repeatedly claimed they

had not taken the earphones and lodged complaints wanting to know how Mrs. Davis could possibly accuse them of
something they hadn't done. I believed their innocence but
asked them to think about the other students they associated
with. The girls were confused with my question, but they did
manage to deny that their friends had anything to do with
their present situation. My rebuttal was to simply ask the
names of their friends.

Without exception, with every name they gave me, I was
able to rattle off offenses each of their friends had committed and the punishments they had been served. I explained
that Mrs. Davis found them guilty by association. Since they
hung around troublemakers, they earned the title of *troublemakers*, even though they weren't. My assumption might have
been accurate, but the girls adamantly denied my explanation.
Whining, they chimed in at the same time yet again, that it
wasn't fair! I agreed but stated that they were dealing with real
people and real-life problems and that meant things weren't
always going to be fair.

Still supporting their claim of innocence, I asked if they
knew who had taken the earphones. Amazingly, not a sound
came from any of them yet they kept shooting side-glances
toward each other. Seeing their response, it was obvious they
knew who had taken the earphones, but I also understood
they would never rat on their friend or friends. I explained to
them that it was obvious they knew who took the earphones
and they needed to clear their names. I offered to help them
but told them they had to start by being honest with me.

Maybe they were just tired of hearing me talk or maybe
I talked some sense into them, but they actually opened up
and admitted they knew not only who stole the earphones
but where they were being kept! I was shocked that they were
holding on to so much information. I quickly expounded that
with the information they were hiding, each of them was
actually guilty by association. Raising my voice just a little for

effect, I reminded them that stealing was not just wrong; it was against the law! Mrs. Davis was right. The police could get involved and their punishment with the police would be much harsher than detention or suspension from school. I tried to drill into their heads that they were dealing with a real crime and that they had better think long and hard about what they needed to do. I definitely got their attention with this rant. I concluded that I would give them a little time to think what they wanted to do, and then we would talk again.

During the time I was busy with the girls, Richard voluntarily helped any of my second or third graders who needed assistance. It was quite heartwarming to see how well he just jumped in to help where needed. When the class period was almost over, not wanting to hurt Richard's feelings, I discretely went around the room looking over my students' completed work to make sure all the work had been done correctly. After surveying all the assignments, I was able to legitimately thank Richard for his incredible help.

During the last period of the day, I asked Richard if he would go to the library with me since I had some apologizing to do, and I wanted him to be with me. He happily agreed. We walked through the library to where Mrs. Davis's office was, and I knocked on her door. We heard an impatient, "Come in!" As we entered the room, it seemed that she was surprised to see us. Getting right to the point, I told her that I knew she was busy, but I needed to apologize for yelling at her when she had come into my room that morning. I admitted that I should never have held such an angry tone with her, and that I would do my best never to let it happen again. I acknowledged that she had a concern with some of my students. I said I would be glad to speak with her in private and at her convenience to work on the problem. Though she was quite short with her response, she did manage to say that eight fifteen the next morning would be good for her. With an upbeat voice, I agreed to the time and repeated that I would be at her office at eight fifteen. Once again, I apologized for the way I had acted earlier, but all she managed to choke out was a quick, "Okay, fine." With that, Richard and I left her office, closing the door behind us.

As we walked back to our room, we were talking about what just happened. The dismissal bell rang so we grabbed Richard's books and continued talking as we headed toward his bus. I thanked Richard for pointing out my poor behavior that morning and for his courage to tell me his feelings. Though I didn't care for Mrs. Davis, I despised my behavior. I was happy to report that apologizing wasn't as hard as I thought it was going to be and was amazed how much better I felt about the whole situation and about myself. With his deep dimpled smile, Richard thanked me for inviting him to witness my apology and said he was relieved I wasn't mad. I assured him that I would never be mad at him as long as he was honest. As he stepped into the bus, I waved goodbye, marveling at what a wonderful person he was and wise beyond his years.

After a night of much needed rest, I was ready to talk with Mrs. Davis and tackle the dilemma with my girls. Heaven must have been smiling on me because the issue with the earphones had already been resolved without me having to get involved! Right before school started, the girls ran into my room and plopped down in their chairs acting as if they were exhausted. It was only eight o'clock. When they got their breath, they sat up in their seats and excitedly explained what happened. They had successfully convinced the boys to return the earphones, which they did as soon as Mrs. Davis opened up the library. Evidently, the boys admitted taking the earphones, apologized for causing so much trouble, and then handed over the earphones. Mrs. Davis accepted their apology and sent them on their way.

I was thrilled the problem had been solved but interestingly, the girls kept chattering. They had an annoying habit of talking over each other where I couldn't understand them. This time, through the garbled mess, they were trying to say that they had told me they hadn't taken the earphones! Though I was glad the problem was resolved, there was still the issue of their choice of friends. All three girls grumbled. I tried to impress upon them the seriousness of what could have happened just because of their association in this situation. They needed to see this as a wakeup call to the type of friends they chose to hang around with. As I always told them, they were wonderful young ladies, and they had worked so hard to make such monumental improvements. It would be a shame if it all went down the drain because they associated with people who continually made poor choices and got into trouble. (At the time, the girls just stared at me like my words were going in one ear and out the other, but weeks later, I noticed they had started doing things with new friends. Thankfully, much better behaving friends!)

After I finished my soap-box spiel, I asked if Mrs. Davis had talked to them about the earphones being returned. In unison, they complained that she had not mentioned anything to them even when she saw them in the library, right before they had come to see me. Mya mumbled that Mrs. Davis just turned away when she saw them. I could see Mrs. Davis doing that, but I wanted to give her the benefit of the doubt and since it was time for me to meet with her, I would find out for myself.

I was at Mrs. Davis's door at exactly eight fifteen. Right on time! I knocked and heard her say a more pleasant, "Come in." When she saw me in the doorway, she responded that we wouldn't have to talk after all. Her demeanor instantly shifted and with an irritated voice, she told me that she had gotten the earphones and the problem was over. Period. She proceeded to look down at the paperwork she had in front of her, totally ignoring the fact that I was still in her office.

Thanks to Richard, this time I kept my cool, even though I wanted to tear into her again. I asked when we could expect her to come to our room. She barely looked up at me but had a puzzled look. I repeated my question. She asked me why in the world she would need to go to my room. I immediately responded that it was imperative that she apologize to my class and to Mya, Morgan, and Toni for her actions the day before. She literally gave a slight giggle of absurdity and said she didn't need to do that because they were probably guilty of something else anyway!

With that comment, I stepped all the way into her office and shut the door, just in case. Thankfully never losing my temper, I admitted that we had a real problem. That got her attention. I summarized her actions and behavior in my class the day before. I repeated, verbatim, what she had accused three innocent girls of doing and how she had unprofessionally interrupted my class. I didn't miss any of the gory details. I admitted that my girls weren't angels, but none of us were. They were, however, human beings wrongly accused of an offense and humiliated in front of their classmates. Then I interjected that if she had come to me in the first place, none of this would have happened. Unfortunately for everyone involved, she had chosen to take things into her own hands. Now she needed to correct her mistake.

I didn't want to have any further discussion, so I ended saying that if she didn't come and apologize, I knew a number of superiors who would be very interested in hearing how she treated my students and me. Begrudgingly, she agreed and muttered a few things I couldn't hear, but I did manage to catch her last comment—"This is ludicrous!"

Since my first class was about to start, she chose to walk back with me. When we entered my room, there were a few students who had nothing to do with this situation. It was a beautiful morning, so I had these students go outside for just a few minutes. Complaining that they didn't understand why they had to leave, they picked up their work, went outside, and sat on the steps.

After I got the students settled outside, I reentered the room and very politely introduced Mrs. Davis. I even bent the truth to help her save face. I explained that the earphones had been returned, and Mrs. Davis agreed that it was important to come speak to all of them. I stepped back and gestured to Mrs. Davis. At first, she stuttered and stammered, but she finally managed to get out that she was wrong about Mya, Morgan, and Toni stealing the earphones. She never actually apologized, but my girls were very gracious and accepted her statement as an apology.

With this done, I had Richard bring in my other students from outside. When everyone was seated, I began talking about their ongoing library assignment. I asked Mrs. Davis to review their assignment since we were so lucky to have her right in our room! She talked a few minutes and answered several really good questions so having her in the room actually turned out to be very helpful for my students. Not surprisingly though, after Mrs. Davis left the trailer, the expected questions were asked. I squelched them immediately, claiming the issue was closed and that we had a great deal of work to catch up on.

When it was time for class to change, Richard came up to me shyly wondering if he could ask one last question about the earphone incident. Since no one was around, I agreed. He merely wanted to know if I thought it was difficult for Mrs. Davis to apologize to the class. I nodded and said, "Absolutely." He then wanted to know why it would be difficult for her since she was the one who was wrong. With a smile, he added that I had only acted poorly. (I loved him for his honesty!) As he looked at me, again with his deep dimples and dark brown eyes, I simply responded that I knew it would be difficult for her because she didn't have the loving support that I had from such a special young man.

Craig

I HAD BEEN working at this school for more than three years, and I had a good working relationship with most of the teachers. They saw that I was not running a daycare center with my class and that I really could help them and our shared students. Many of the teachers learned that I was totally committed to the students and would do anything I could to help them. Because of this reputation, Mrs. Cameron came to see me about Craig, a new student she had in her room. Mrs. Cameron was the fourth grade teacher who helped me with Donny when he returned the materials I had borrowed. According to her, Craig was functioning far below grade level, and she believed he was behind not because of missed instruction but because he could not seem to grasp the concepts being taught. Mrs. Cameron described him as being a very enthusiastic and happy child but could see frustration setting in and wanted to help him but wasn't sure what to do.

I told Mrs. Cameron I would be happy to help so I began by getting permission from Craig's parents to observe him in his regular classroom and work with him a few times one-on-one. Every time I worked with Craig, it was obvious he was a happy child and had an attitude of excitement for school.

Mrs. Cameron had described Craig perfectly and had accurately pinpointed so many of his troubled areas. His drive to learn was heartwarming but unfortunately, he was not able to retain much of what he was taught. Something had to be done to help him. I knew we had to get a jump on assisting Craig because, just as Mrs. Cameron had already noticed, frustration was a new element for him, and we didn't want it to dampen his drive.

I knew the placement process was very slow due to all the required observations, paperwork, and conferences. It would be months before Craig would get help and that was just not soon enough. I told Mrs. Cameron I would take Craig even without formal papers being issued for placement because I knew that since he hadn't even been referred, we were looking at about four months or more of lag time from start to finish to get him in my room. As long as Mrs. Cameron approved and I had Craig's parents' consent, I would go ahead and start working with him immediately. The red tape charade was just not worth waiting for when he needed help quickly.

I had never met Craig's parents, but I had talked with Mrs. Millner to get her permission prior to observing Craig in his classroom. From what Craig described to me, I knew his mom and his dad both worked but still struggled to make ends meet. It was obvious from all the stories Craig told me that both parents took a great deal of pride and responsibility for their children despite their lack of funds. According to Craig, he had three siblings, and all four of them got along very well. He always spoke highly of his parents and talked about all the wonderful family activities they would do together. He came from and enjoyed a happy family life. Just that alone was so different from many of my other students; it was refreshing to hear all the time that was spent together as a family. Because of the good things I heard about Craig's parents, I was looking forward to our conference.

Craig was accurate with his description of his mom. What

a wonderful person. I spoke very candidly about the concerns Mrs. Cameron and I had for Craig. I offered some suggestions, one being that we could begin the process to get Craig placed in my class. Mrs. Millner was nodding and smiling as I was explaining the purpose of my room and how I might be able to help Craig. Then, I explained the time it would take to have all the papers and documentation completed to have Craig enter my class. As I was telling Mrs. Millner the time frame involved, I saw her smile fade, and she became very quiet. It was obvious that she had no idea it would take so long to get help for her son. With her permission, I could get the ball rolling but unfortunately, it was a slow-moving ball.

During this meeting, I learned that Mrs. Millner was also suffering from guilt. She said she knew Craig was having trouble long before this. When he was in the first grade, she questioned the teacher about his lack of progress compared to the progress of her three older children when they were in the first grade. The only insight the teacher gave her was that children learn differently and not to compare Craig to his siblings. From that point on, Mrs. Millner felt she should let the school do what they thought was best, even though deep down she knew there was a real problem brewing with Craig's learning process. Then, apparently because of Craig's sweet personality, the school's teachers let him just slide by with very low expectations. It wasn't until the Millner family moved and enrolled Craig in our school that his obvious lack of educational progress was brought back to light.

When I finished explaining all that was involved in officially enrolling him, I explained that the time frame was far too long to wait so what I wanted from her was verbal permission allowing me to start immediately. I would just need a few days to prepare materials for him. I also needed to coordinate with his regular classroom teacher to find times when he could attend my class and then begin. As I was telling her what I was offering to do, her eyes filled with tears, and she was nodding her head in approval. I tried to reassure her that with the continued love and support she and her husband were giving Craig and the new help the school could offer him, I felt sure we would see progress. The downside to this arrangement was that on days I was not present (which was practically never) or when any administration personnel would be in my room, Craig would have to stay in his regular class. The other downside was that on the off chance Craig was not approved, he would not be able to continue in my class. Thankfully, none of this deterred her from allowing me to move forward with Craig.

Mrs. Millner had regained her composure and verbally gave me her permission. As we were wrapping up our meeting, she shook my hand vigorously and kept saying how grateful she and her husband were to Mrs. Cameron and me for offering to help her son. It seemed odd to hear that because, after all, we were there to help, but I knew what she meant. I thanked her also for caring as she and her husband did and for being so dedicated to helping Craig. I added that I wished more parents would get so involved.

I told Mrs. Millner that officially, we never had this meeting since there were no official papers to enroll Craig at this point. I did have all the observation and referral paperwork properly completed and signed so I knew I wasn't doing anything *really* wrong; I was just speeding up the process to help a child.

Craig started in my class three days after I met with Mrs. Millner, but it took just over four months to have him *officially* enrolled. I know I broke a rule for placement but realizing what Craig accomplished over the unofficial time period in my class, it would have been almost criminal to have made him wait to get help. I know there have to be guidelines and rules to help properly place children, but I also believe much of the red tape could and should be streamlined so children could get help faster.

Color of Skin

BEKAH, A TIMID and gentle third grader, and I were having the best time talking about the story we were reading while the rest of the class was busy with their independent work. As we were chatting, I heard the crackling noise of an upcoming announcement over our P.A. system. When I heard the person's voice, I cringed. It was my least favorite person in the school, the principal! He had the volume of the system way too high so at first it surprised my students and me when his voice thundered into our classroom. He quickly and unapologetically barked out my name and immediately requested the race and gender numbers of all my students! Yes, he was that blunt and that thoughtless.

I was irritated that this man was interrupting my class and also infuriated at the subject matter of his interruption, so I didn't respond immediately. I was actually trying to find an adequate way to answer him. He didn't like the pause, so with an annoyed tone, he asked if I'd heard him. I acknowledged that I had heard his request and asked if he could turn the volume down so I could hear him better. *Off* would have been the best choice but that wasn't going to be possible. I told him I would get the information by the end of my lunch period.

He growled a most demeaning question, "Don't you already know the breakdown of your students?" I was not ashamed to say that I didn't.

I don't know whether I was different from teachers in other schools but evidently the ones in this school knew their numbers by memory or had them written down to be easily retrieved. When the principal heard I didn't have the information immediately available, he demanded that I get it to him as soon as possible. Using the nicest voice I could without sounding too insincere, I let him know that I had classes until lunch, and *then* I would get him that information. He snapped back demanding to get the information ASAP. All I could choke out was, "Yes, sir."

I know I could have gotten the information to him much earlier than by the end of lunch, but there were several reasons I didn't. First, I just plain didn't like this man, and I resented how he treated my students and me, but the biggest reason I didn't move faster was because of Bekah. I definitely didn't want her to feel like she wasn't my priority or that what we were doing wasn't important. I also didn't want her to think that the numbers of boys to girls and blacks to whites was worthy of my immediate attention.

Maybe this information seemed foreign to me since I worked with students on specific areas for short periods of time. Color and gender were never important. I didn't have set groups, bathroom lines, or recess play groups that might call for the need to have a balanced ratio of boys to girls. Color, I still don't understand that one.

When my students left for lunch, I sat looking at my class list. I mentally saw students with pale skin and brown eyes, dark skin with green eyes, light skin with curly hair, and dark skin with straight hair. It seemed sad that they had to be put in categories when they were such individuals. I went down my list and thought about each child. Aaden was very quiet, very sensitive, loved to draw and loved to tell jokes. Derrick was a meticulous worker, loved to build, enjoyed reading Super-man comics and played well with other children. Colton had a great dry sense of humor, had an inner drive to always do well, constantly absorbed anything related to science, had a few close friends but got along with everyone. Bekah was very tentative meeting new people, relished being read to, loved to talk with her friends, and enjoyed singing even though she couldn't carry a tune!

I did this with my whole class list. Gender and race had nothing to do with how I taught them or how I treated them. I saw how diverse all my students were and yet I was asked to melt them down into two insignificant categories. They were such individuals to me. The only real categories important to me were their needs and wants. Children need and want pretty much the same things, which are love, attention, and direction. Since students are always in different stages with different personalities, successful teachers must be creative to reach them where they are. Knowing their gender and race won't help.

I don't mean to be simplistic about this topic, but if adults wouldn't make gender and race an issue, it wouldn't be an issue for children. Children really don't care. As long as the child sitting by them is nice and treats them well, the children get along just fine. The teacher I replaced definitely made gender and race issues so when I first started teaching, we had many needless conflicts because an adult had taught them that these issues were important. It took a while to defuse this misguided thought, but over time, all my students dropped the race and gender card as an excuse for their behavior and attitudes.

Bekah summed up my feelings quite well. After the inci-dent with the principal abruptly interrupting our class, Bekah had asked why he had to know that information. I briefly explained what the numbers meant and how they were used to control student enrollment in classes and in schools. (I with-held telling her that was also how schools got some money.)

She was silent for a short while, but I could tell she was in deep thought. Then, she broke her silence by asking what the break-downs were. I showed her the numbers of the two categories. Bekah noted that I had more boys and more blacks. Since she was one of my newest students, she asked me if she had been a boy or black would she have been allowed in my room. I tentatively replied that I wasn't sure but probably not. Bekah got really quiet again but then, almost like something struck a nerve in her, she blurted out that it wasn't fair! Immediately, she pointed to another new student in our room and said she couldn't imagine class without him. I agreed whole-heartedly with her. Our class just wouldn't have been the same without Craig!

Mrs. MacGregor

I HAD WORKED with Colton for three years and was thrilled with all of his progress. At the close of his second grade, it was obvious that academically, Colton was progressing wonderfully, and he only needed me for encouragement and consistent nudges to stay on track. School life was looking so good for Colton.

At the end of each school year, the principal would make class assignments for the following year. Even though I had little respect for him, I appreciated the fact that he always allowed me to assist with the placement of my students, mainly matching personalities, so the teacher and student could have the best year possible together. This year, we had a new principal, for whom I grew to have a great deal of respect. Unfortunately, we didn't start off very well. He didn't support or allow special classroom placement for my students because he thought it gave an unfair advantage to them and not the other students in the school. I strongly disagreed, reasoning that my students already had many strikes against them within the school system. I believed individual attention to class placement for my students was one step closer to making things more equitable. Since the vast majority of the teachers were very good, I chose a wide variety of teachers for their particular personalities and their willingness to be flexible with my program and my students.

Mrs. MacGregor was the exception to all the other teachers. There is no other way to describe her teaching skills other than to say she was absolutely horrible! I ached for all her students because their third grade year was going to be an absolute waste of time. All I could hope for them was that they wouldn't experience too much damage over that nine-month period. Mrs. MacGregor was always yelling at her students, whether she was in her class or out in the halls. The yelling only seemed to ignite the students' poor behavior because her students were routinely unruly and unfortunately never seemed happy. This was a teacher I made sure none of my students ever had because they all needed order and consistency. Her class was no class for any of them.

During a conversation with the principal, I brought up the subject of student placement. He said the assignments had been completed and that I could look at the list. Scrutinizing the names, I was actually pleased seeing where he had put my students until I saw Mrs. MacGregor's class. Near the end of her list was my precious Colton's name! That was the worst possible placement for him. Colton already had to repeat first grade and he definitely didn't need any more problems to interfere with his progress. He was feeling so confident and happy in his well-structured classes that offered him peace and quiet. I knew Colton was still easily rattled with chaotic noise. I couldn't imagine what would happen to him in this class for a whole school year.

I asked the principal if I could move any of the students if there was a real problem. Before I finished my sentence, he answered with a strong and unmoving, "No!" He explained that he merely showed me the list so I could begin talking to the teachers about my students. I knew I had no leg to stand on so I didn't push the issue, but I also knew I would solve the problem one way or another. At the time, I had no idea how I would do that but solve it, I did!

Technically, what I did was wrong, and I could have possibly gotten into a great deal of trouble if I had been caught, but fortunately, I wasn't caught. I didn't get into trouble, and Colton was saved from a disastrous year. For me, I did what I had to do and actually, the situation presented itself. I just took advantage of it.

During a teacher workday, prior to the first day of school, I went to see the principal in his office. On a very rare occasion, no one was in the office, including the principal. Wanting to deliver information to him, I wrote a note and went into his office to leave it on his desk. As I was I placing the note down, I saw that the class assignment list was right on top of his desk. Without questioning my actions, though my heart was pounding the whole time, I got a pencil, flipped through the pages until I found Mrs. MacGregor's list. I quickly erased Colton's name and wrote it on Mrs. Galloway's list. Her class was not full, and I thought she would be good at helping Colton get out of his serious shell with her wonderful sense of humor and well-organized style. I wrote in such a way that my writing looked similar to the other names on the list. Mrs. MacGregor needed one less student, and Mrs. Galloway would thoroughly enjoy Colton (and I was right!).

The next day, we had a large faculty meeting where the lists were distributed to the teachers. I made sure I sat next to Mrs. Galloway. Holding my breath, I looked at her list and sure enough, there was Colton's name!

Colton's year with Mrs. Galloway was absolutely marvelous. The two of them got along so well. Not only did Mrs. Galloway help Colton loosen up a little and have some fun, she continued building his confidence. At the end of the year, I found it quite funny that Mrs. Galloway remarked to me that she couldn't have imagined the year without Colton and stated how lucky she was to have gotten him placed in her room. I smiled and said I was glad she felt that way. Little did she know luck had nothing to do with it!

Purpose for Reading

LIFE IN MY classroom would have been much easier if I had more students like Shane Overby. I felt fortunate though to have had him as a student for three wonderful years. Personally, I didn't feel he needed to be in my room since I believed the root of his problem stemmed from his home life, but official educational testing showed otherwise, and he was labeled with a mild learning disability. Because of the results of this testing, he was placed in my room. Maybe he shouldn't have been labeled learning disabled, but I believe he and I needed each other.

Shane was average in height but he had a small and frail build for his eight years, and he was far from being coordinated. His skin was so pale it almost looked translucent and his head was extremely round and covered with blond curly hair. Shane's most striking feature was his eyes. Not only were they huge blue eyes with long lashes, they were quite penetrating with a type of yearning in them. His eyes seemed to say he was looking for more. More of what, I was never sure, but he always seemed to be longing for *something*.

Shane was a captivating student who challenged my teaching skills every day in ways no other student had.

Teachers who worked with him before me described him as shy, but I didn't. He was just quiet. When he wanted to talk, he did. When he didn't want to talk, he didn't. Plus, if he didn't have something good to say, he didn't say anything. During some of his quiet moments, he seemed to be soaking up what he heard and saw going on around him. Shane seemed to only have two moods. Usually, he was in a good mood, but if he was not, he was just sad. On those occasions, I was probably affected more than he was. He had such a gentle spirit it was painful to see him so miserable.

He worked diligently to do a good job with all of his classwork. Though he had a bit of trouble with math, it was nothing out of the ordinary for an average third grader. His reading was what gave him minor troubles, comprehension to be specific. As I worked with Shane, I believed if he could read something that interested him, his reading comprehension would improve, giving him a boost in confidence. The stories he was expected to read in his regular classroom were long and extremely boring. It is hard to teach anything to students if they are not interested in the topic being taught, learning disability or not. When they are bored, most of the time students' efforts will fade, and their attention will wander. Shane was no exception. When we would try to do his assignments from his classroom, his mind would start wandering soon after we started reading the assigned story. It was torture for both of us getting through the story and answering the questions. The assignments seemed to have no purpose and were very dry. It was always a relief when we'd complete the work in his reader because then we could choose a book from the ones I had in my room. They always had an interesting storyline and were fun to read. This was when we had so many memorable times together. Shane had no trouble paying attention, understanding the story, and answering detailed questions during these times.

I didn't set out to have a wide variety of reading material

in my room. I wish I had. My collection of books just grew as I brought in books to meet the needs of each of my students. The books I had in the room were on many different topics and on many different reading levels, allowing students to choose from a wide variety of options. Shane would choose books about adventure, history, and mystery. Anything that had a good story was fine with him. Though we had a great deal of fun reading a variety of books, I knew I wanted to find something for him that was more than just acceptable. I wanted him to be hungry for the subject. I continued my search for something that really interested Shane. I kept bringing in new books, which he always enjoyed, but there was no spark, so the search continued.

I scoured the school library and the public library and checked out all types of books on all types of subjects. He would read and enjoy them but still no spark. No hunger for more. I decided to take him to the school library during his sessions with me hoping he would spot something he liked. No such luck.

The reason I worked so hard doing this with Shane was that one of the keys to success I had with my older students was finding their particular area of interest and then teaching the skills they needed using that topic as my springboard. Improvements were always faster and greater if I could do this, and I believed it would work for Shane. I just had the frustrating job of finding a topic that captured his heart.

As with so many other situations, with time and patience, the student would actually show me the answer to the problem, so then I could help him or her. One day Shane came into my room for class, placed his books on his desk, and sat down. All very normal for him. It wasn't until he gave a heavy, pitiful sigh that I even noticed something might be wrong. He'd slumped over his desk holding his head up with his hands. He gave a deep sigh again and said under his breath, "I give up." That was definitely not normal for

Shane. As soon as I finished with the student I was helping, I went over to talk with him. By that time, he was just gazing out the window, holding his head with one arm and quietly tapping his fingers on the desk with the other. I pulled up a chair, sat down beside him, and cheerfully asked how his day was. He looked at me, simply turned away and then in the most pitiful voice said "Okay." This was definitely not my Shane. We had such a good relationship that on any other day, I would have gotten all types of details from the beginning of the day to that very moment. "Okay" was never a response Shane would give me, so I knew there was a problem. I rephrased my question and asked what happened that morning. No response. I just got *a look*. So, I rephrased my question and asked what happened in class. He looked at me again, turned away and while looking out the window, choked out, "Nothing."

It was the last class of the day on a Friday. All my energy from the week and the day was gone. My tolerance and willingness to play the child psychology game was also long gone, so I admitted it. I just blurted out that I was no good at the game Twenty Questions and would he please just tell me what was bugging him! He looked straight into my eyes, with that look of pain and sadness, showed a glimmer of a smile on his face and uttered, "Oh, Miss Chandler," and turned away. There was a moment of silence and then finally while Shane was still looking out the window, he took a deep breath and with a broken voice told me that the kids in his class had been making fun of him. Then he got quiet again. I felt like someone had impaled a dagger in my heart as I witnessed the pain Shane was feeling and so desperately trying to hide. In my loving, yet obnoxious way, I coaxed him to tell me more. He still was not looking at me, but I could see tears welling up in his eyes. He explained that during his reading class, he and his classmates were reading about horses and unicorns. He had raised his hand, which he usually never did in his regular classroom, and the teacher had called on him. According to Shane, he told a mini story about a horse that had wings and proudly shared that his dad had told him all about this horse. I am not sure what was so different between the mythical unicorn and what Shane described, but evidently the kids laughed and made fun of him.

This was such a difficult situation for Shane. First of all, he was extremely sensitive. In addition to being sensitive, he was protective of his father. Shane came from divorced parents and rarely saw his dad, though he thought the world of him. I could see that he was struggling to internalize the fact that he and a very special story his dad had told him had been ridiculed. Despite his efforts to hide his emotions, Shane had to blink and his tears overflowed. He quickly turned his back to me, trying unsuccessfully to hide his tears. I gave him a gentle hug as I whispered that his classmates had no right to laugh at him because his father was right and there was such a story about a mythical creature as he was told.

I was startled when Shane whirled around, obviously not caring about his tear-soaked face any more and stared right at me with a questioning look. As I repeated myself, explaining that there were wonderful tales about a mighty winged horse, his expression slowly changed to joyful disbelief. I realized I had unintentionally given him something more valuable than money—dignity for himself and pride in his father.

I began telling him the background I knew about the Greek mythological creature, Pegasus. In order to describe this wonderful stallion properly, I had to introduce a few other mythical characters. Shane was genuinely intrigued and asked wonderful questions. I couldn't talk fast enough for him. Many of his questions I couldn't answer specifically, so I told him we would need to look them up together. This was the beginning of a wonderful adventure for Shane and me. At last, through all the time, struggle, and pain, I finally found something that created a fire in Shane: Greek mythology.

Every session from then on, Shane and I would first complete the assignments from his regular class, then we would delve into a new story in a Greek mythology book that was on his reading level that I'd found at the public library. The stories were quite captivating, and the pictures were equally dramatic. We always read the stories aloud, so many times other students would come over and listen to the story. We had many marvelous class discussions, and Shane loved the fact that he was the center of attention since these were *his* stories everyone was discussing.

Over time, the other students' interest lessened, so I made a Greek mythology reading nook for just Shane and me. This thrilled Shane even more. The nook was quite simple. It was in the back corner of the trailer in between two small bookcases, giving us about three feet to scrunch in together with fun pillows I had brought in to sit on. It may have been simple and tiny but it was our spot.

We would read as many books as we could find on the subject that were on or near Shane's reading ability. One book that he brought in was excellent, but it was way above his reading level, so we agreed that he would read the captions to the pictures and I would read the stories. Whichever book we read, Shane always had to answer comprehension questions about the story when I was finished reading. That was never a problem. He held on to every word I read, and if he didn't understand something as I read it, he would ask me to explain what was going on because he *wanted* to understand. This young boy had no comprehension problem. He understood the vast majority of what he read and heard. He just would mentally shut down when he was bored or not interested.

As with so many of my other students, Shane's reading skills progressed much faster and his confidence increased once he found reading material that interested him. He was successful at reading what he enjoyed so with his increased confidence, over time, he started doing much better with his comprehension of other topics that were not necessarily interesting to him. I believed then, as I still do today, that Shane didn't have a comprehension problem; the educational system did.

There are such wonderful classic stories our children could be reading, but where are they? You'll be hard pressed to find them in children's books or in the classrooms. Most reading textbooks have modern stories about today's so called social problems and are just simply boring. Stories should have excitement, adventure, a reason for reading them, and a reason for remembering them. They should be fun.

I know it is no fault of children when they struggle to follow along with some of the stories they are asked to read. I zone out myself when I read them, and I doubt I would do well on comprehension questions. Educators and parents alike are not providing our children reading material that is worth reading. We are not giving them a reason to learn to love reading. We have successfully made reading a chore instead of a pleasure. It seems that the stories and books students read are all socially or politically correct. We find fault with children when they don't comprehend information that the school system feels they are supposed to comprehend, yet we don't ever seem to consider the fact that maybe, just maybe, we are the ones at fault, and we are the ones failing. Unfortunately, it is our children who are suffering from our failure.

Mitchell

MITCHELL WAS AN obnoxious child. He was loud, rude, and always tried to be the class clown. Mitchell was placed in my program when he was in the fourth grade. He proved to be an annoying and sometimes impossible child to work with even one-on-one. It wasn't surprising then to hear that in a classroom setting, he succeeded in totally exasperating Mrs. Moore, his regular classroom teacher. Neither of us seemed to make any significant academic progress with Mitchell since his disruptive behavior took all of our time. He was easily distracted, couldn't stay in his seat or sit still, constantly blurted out inappropriate comments, and basically interrupted class many time throughout the day. Sadly, it was a real challenge just to like Mitchell, let alone teach him!

Mrs. Moore and I both knew Mitchell was smart because on rare occasions we would see glimpses of what he was capable of doing and learning. Normally, this only happened when we were able to get him away from other students though his behavior would still be irritating. With other students near, academics went down the drain, and his behavior was simply infuriating. It wasn't hard to understand that if teachers had a challenging time getting along with Mitchell, his classmates would also have troubles accepting him. Unfortunately, not only did his classmates not like him, they liked to make fun of him.

The other classmates may have used Mitchell's curly red hair, massive freckles, or robust size in jokes, but the ridicule seemed to stem from the fact that Mitchell was just not like-able! It was terrible to see how cruel the other students were to him and how obvious most of Mitchell's behavior was to divert the pain, hurt, and humiliation caused by the other students' actions. The teachers and I were able to stop the torment toward Mitchell when we were in the immediate area, but when we were not in the vicinity, he was prime for unrelenting ridicule.

Granted, some of Mitchell's behavioral issues came from the teasing, but it was difficult to put a finger on what was causing all of Mitchell's extremely poor behavior. On one hand, Mitchell tested and was diagnosed as gifted and talented in math. On the other hand, he was found to have a severe learning disability with reading. Adding insult to injury, with these two contrasting academic diagnoses, Mitchell was officially labeled as having ADHD, attention deficit hyperactivity disorder!

Initially, I thought Mitchell's root cause of his irritating behavior was not from his academic struggles but because of prejudice and bullying. There are laws all over the country that protect people from being discriminated against because of sex, race, or creed but nothing protects a person from being discriminated against because of weight. Overweight people, adults or children, are probably the most misunderstood and most discriminated against population. Weight was a serious problem for Mitchell. I believed much of his poor behavior was a reaction to the teasing and his attempt to hold on to whatever dignity he could. Weight was a significant part of his problem, but the real issue was actually much more difficult to uncover.

Instead of placing Mitchell in the gifted and talented class where he could have been challenged in math, he was placed solely in my resource room to work on his reading. Also, because of his hyperactivity, Mitchell had been put on Ritalin, which the pediatrician believed would make him calm, pliable, and attentive.

As I have already admitted, I abhor the use of behavior-altering medication with children. I despise it even more when that medication is the first solution used to correct a child's unpopular behavior. Before a child should ever be put on a behavior-altering medication, he or she should go through rigorous changes in lifestyle first. Briefly, without getting on my soap box for too long again, I believe a child should be checked to see if he or she is simply getting proper and regular hours of sleep. Lack of sleep alone could cause a child to have difficulty with attention and behavior. Then a child needs to have a healthy diet, get plenty of exercise, and have limited technological influence such as TV, computer use, Xbox, phones, etc. Then the issue of home life, which is a touchy subject, absolutely must be considered. No child can concentrate or behave normally if the home life is not a peaceful and happy place.

Any one of these issues that is out of whack can cause a child to exhibit serious emotional and behavioral problems. Children need and depend on the adults in their world to keep these areas in their life stable. Unfortunately, in this fast-paced world where the easy fix is to just pop a pill, children suffer. I may have been wrong with my first explanation of bullying being the cause for Mitchell's behavior, but at least I was trying to find the *why* causing his hyperactivity and poor behavior instead of just covering up the problem with a pill.

One afternoon, while in the P.E. teacher's office, I picked up a health magazine, and a particular article caught my eye. This article was discussing symptoms adults and children might have if they had food allergies. As I read the article,

the behaviors and problems the author cited sounded as if he
had used Mitchell as his example. Everything he described as
a symptom of food allergies, Mitchell exhibited! Could a food
allergy be Mitchell's problem? How could I go about testing
my new hypothesis? And, how in the world was I going to
take this new idea to his mother?

Through the two years I had been working with Mitchell, I had only met his mother. His father was present in the
family; he just never came to the parent/teacher conferences.
Mrs. Portland was a devoted, supportive, and loving mother
to both of her children. Mitchell was the older at ten years
old and the daughter was four years younger. Though it was
obvious both children were loved, it seemed like the daughter
was doted on by the parents since she was petite, quite pretty,
and very sweet. In regard to academics, both children were
showing signs of difficulty in school so the mom had taken
them for testing. Unfortunately for Mitchell, he was the only
one to exhibit real learning challenges. His sister's problems
just seemed to stem from the fact that she was spoiled.

Mitchell had been on Ritalin for one year prior to coming
to our school and entering my program. In the doctor's report,
he claimed that Mitchell would "probably" grow out of his
hyperactivity as he got older. (This doctor did not document or
tell the mom that staying on Ritalin into puberty could cause
Mitchell some life-changing health problems.) Over the year
that Mitchell had been on this drug, there was no documentation to show whether or not it was benefiting him. The only
thing recorded was that the doses kept getting stronger, and
the reason given for the higher doses was that Mitchell was
growing (ballooning was more like it)!

In his files, I couldn't find any reference to Mitchell's
extreme weight gain. When I pursued the issue of weight with
Mrs. Portland, she just laughed and said that her husband was
a large man, and Mitchell must have inherited his "huskiness."
Her husband might have been husky, I don't know as I never

saw him, but Mitchell was on the verge of being obese at the young age of ten!

Holding on to the possibilities of a food allergy affecting Mitchell, my challenge now was to work with the mom, who chose to turn a blind-eye to the obvious weight issue, and convince her to consider my new hypothesis of possible food allergies. I felt this was going to be quite challenging since Mitchell was already on a program under the guidance of his pediatrician and a behavior specialist. Here I was, with no background in the area of food allergies and only a few years under my belt in actual teaching experience. Just because of a hunch I had, I was going to try to convince this mother to pursue a totally different direction and head mostly into the unknown since diagnosing food allergies was a difficult undertaking.

Whom would you follow? Would you follow the medical professionals who had a solid case to support their diagnosis and treatment? Or would you follow a teacher, a relatively new one at that, who admitted being baffled by the whole situation and offered an unproven direction to seek out possibly a different diagnosis using no medication? I would choose to follow the doctors! Luckily for Mitchell, I wasn't his mom, because Mrs. Portland chose to follow my idea and me. Our meeting and conversation appeared to be a welcomed relief for her because she admitted that she never liked the course she was taking with the doctors, but she didn't know what else to do!

Under the supervision of his pediatrician, Mitchell began the slow process of being weaned off of the Ritalin. In the meantime, I had to work with Mitchell's classroom teacher to help her adjust to Mitchell being off his medication. And then, of course, I had to learn to handle Mitchell myself. (Granted, the medicine did make him calm and pliable, but it was obvious the medicine's effect was just temporary.)

Though his classroom teacher and I had our challenges

with Mitchell's unmasked behavior, which was now full-blown disruptive behavior, the hardest job truly landed on Mrs. Portland. His regular classroom teacher and I had to handle Mitchell a few hours a day. Mrs. Portland had to deal with Mitchell's erratic behavior much longer than we did. Though she never complained, I always wondered if she had ever second-guessed her decision to take Mitchell off of the medication. In addition to struggling with Mitchell's unleashed behavior, Mrs. Portland also had to take him back and forth to the allergy specialist. Test after test was given to him to see if he had sensitivity to anything that might cause Mitchell's hyperactivity.

I am grateful to Mrs. Portland for her determination and willingness to go through all this to actually find the answer. After several months, the testing showed that Mitchell not only had an allergy to something, he had a severe reaction when exposed to it. Amazingly, his allergy was to any type of food preservative. No wonder the kid was flying high all the time! Mitchell's main diet was processed meats and processed foods.

With this new information, Mitchell and the rest of the family went on a strict lifestyle change eliminating preservatives in their diets. This was probably a huge challenge for the entire family, but lo and behold, Mitchell's behavior began to improve! His parents, classroom teacher, and I had to help him unlearn some bad behavior that he had developed while under the influence of the preservatives but that was the easy part. We were working with a smart and now rational child who understood what we were trying to accomplish.

Over the next year, I was thrilled to watch Mitchell do much better in school. As he improved, he was able to stay longer in his regular classroom and needed me less and less. With Mitchell's improved behavior, he actually started attending the gifted and talented program (which was now run by a fabulous and challenging new teacher)!

I couldn't have been happier with Mitchell's academic gains, but I was disappointed with several things that didn't change as much as I had hoped. Though Mitchell was preservative free and eating much healthier foods, he didn't lose much weight. Mitchell managed to make a few friends, but sadly many of his classmates still teased him. I guess a bright side to the teasing was that at least now he was able to stand up for himself in a healthier manner.

I wish I had been able to get more students off the medication they were on for hyperactivity, but at least Mitchell was saved from being filled with unnecessary and potentially harmful chemicals. I did find it odd that after the hyperactivity issue was solved, Mitchell was still an obnoxious student and a pain in the neck to work with, but this time it was the *real* Mitchell, and I couldn't help but love him!

Abigail's Circus

TO AN OUTSIDER, it seemed I was very lucky being a resource teacher since usually I only received four to five new students at the beginning of each school year. The way my program worked was that though a student moved up a grade, he or she continued attending my program year after year. Since my roster was always full, the only way I could get new students was when my current students advanced into what is now called middle school or their families moved out of our school district. Because of this system, I had the benefit of already knowing most of my students, their needs, learning methods, and personalities. That meant I could start the new school year right where we left off with just a brief review. It was great since there was so little time wasted getting to know all my students and figuring them out.

Yes, from an outsider's view, I may have looked lucky but anyone who understood the students who were in my program knew I had a great deal of work with each new student. There was actually a mathematical equation to compute the student load I could carry. The actual disability and the severity of it carried a number. Depending on the disability, each child I had to teach would consume as much time (or more) as working with three to four students without any disabilities.

So, receiving four to five new students a year was like twelve to twenty new students in addition to the other twenty-some returning students. Those returning students were already equivalent to sixty or more students! With every student, I had more reports and paperwork required. Plus, I had additional meetings with faculty, school officials, and parents on a continual basis. Then, in addition to working with the requirements stated in the official I.E.P. (Individual Educational Program) of the new or returning students, I developed my own individual lesson plan for each student and updated it daily.

Starting my fourth full year teaching, Abigail was one of my new students who came into my program and into my life. In my opinion, she was an incredibly happy and beautiful child. Her eyes were bright and her smile contagious. When she smiled, the whole world seemed to smile with her. Abigail came from a very poor home life. Note I did not say family life. I never did find out who exactly lived with Abigail or if the people in her house were even related to her. There was a person or people who looked after her because though her clothes were old, she came to school clean and tidy.

Abigail was in the first grade but in placement only. She was still having trouble with letters, their sounds, and their names while her classmates were reading the primers and writing their own grade level stories. She may have loved the social side of school but every day was a struggle academically.

Abigail and I were so lucky to have Mrs. Schmitt as her regular classroom teacher. Mrs. Schmitt handled Abigail in such a positive and professional way in her class and always gave an incredible amount of time and effort to work with me. Together, Mrs. Schmitt and I made a very effective team for Abigail. It always amazed me to see how much was accomplished with a student when people involved with that student

worked together without egos and power struggles getting in
the way. In Abigail's case, neither of us worried about anything other than what was best for Abigail. Any student I
had from Mrs. Schmitt's room was at my door on time for
class, and Abigail was no exception. She was also no exception
needing help outside of school.

The Barnum and Bailey Circus was in town and was the
hot topic among many of my young students. Overhearing
these discussions, I learned that Abigail had never been to a
circus and that she desperately wanted to go someday because
she had to see the elephants. I can't remember how I got myself
into the situation, but I'm sure Abigail did some fast-talking,
and I was too soft to say anything other than "Yes." All I knew
was that Abigail and I were going to the Barnum and Bailey
Circus Friday, which was four days away.

I had to get a permission slip signed in order to take
Abigail, and I knew that was not going to be easy since no
one at school ever really knew for certain who lived with Abigail. Normally, Abigail's grandmother, her official guardian,
was the person I would communicate with regarding Abigail,
but she was never dependable with short notice. Since I didn't
have time to track down the grandmother, I simply sent the
note home with Abigail hoping someone would sign it. Sure
enough, Abigail brought the slip back the next day, and it was
signed. I have no idea what relation the person who signed the
permission slip was to Abigail, but she shared Abigail's last
name. All I knew was that the principal approved our fieldtrip
and that meant Abigail and I were going to the circus.

In order to take Abigail that Friday, I also had to tell her
bus driver, Mr. Hales. Abigail came to school on a special mini
bus that many of my students rode. I needed to let him know
that she would not be riding his bus home on Friday since I
would be taking her home after we went to the circus.

Mr. Hales took meticulous care of his young riders. He
was very much a grandfather-type person, but he was also

very strict and extremely stubborn. He was always happy and cordial but one thing was for sure, Mr. Hales always got the last word. He listened to me about my plans for Abigail and nodded, agreeing that the circus sounded great but stated under no circumstance was I going to be taking her home. He declared that he would drive her home. Totally taking over the conversation, Mr. Hales explained that I had no business driving in that part of town, especially at that time of night, by myself. Instead, he told me that I was to call him when the circus was over, and he would come and get Abigail and take her home. Knowing it was my responsibility to return her home, I emphatically stated that I had to go along too. He didn't like the idea, but he had known me long enough to understand I was just as stubborn as he was, so he begrudgingly agreed. Par for the course, Mr. Hales made sure he got the last word as he grumbled how much he didn't like me coming along.

Friday morning, Abigail bounced into my room like a Super Ball. Her excitement was uncontainable. Without question, schoolwork for her was all about the circus. I am sure for Abigail, the day probably seemed like it would never end. The day felt long for Mrs. Schmitt and me too but for different reasons. Abigail drove us crazy with her constant questions like "What time is it?" "Is it time to go yet?" "When are we going to leave?" Couple her endless questions with her magnified inability to concentrate, and it made for a very long day! But if truth be told, we both loved seeing her genuine excitement.

When the final bell rang, Abigail was on my doorstep ready to go. It was only three thirty, and the circus didn't start until six. Knowing I would have a large block of time to fill, I had decided that we would get dinner before we got to the circus. I knew we would be hungry, but I also needed to keep her busy. Locking the door to my trailer, I told her she got to choose where we went for dinner. After I gave her several choices, she chose pizza. The choice of pizza didn't surprise me, but what shocked me was that she had never had pizza before.

As we walked to the teachers' parking lot, Abigail yelled out to all the children we passed, as they waited for their buses, that she, Abigail, was going to ride in Miss Chandler's car, get pizza, and go to the circus. She hopped and skipped, swinging my arm all the way to my car.

I never figured out exactly why I didn't encounter jealousy with my students. All my children knew I was taking Abigail and no one else, yet no one complained of favoritism. All my other students had been to the circus but Abigail hadn't, so maybe they thought it was only fair that she was getting to go. I never kept secrets from my students. I consistently told them exactly what I was doing and why. Maybe being up front and honest was the key.

Before we arrived at the restaurant, I explained to Abigail exactly how much money I had to spend for dinner. Even though I knew she had no concept of the value of money, I had to make sure she knew there was a limited amount of it. I also clarified that any leftover money from dinner would leave money to spend at the circus. Abigail listened intently and seemed to understand what I was saying. She especially liked the idea of having money to spend at the circus.

At the pizza parlor, we discussed what we wanted on our pizza and what we wanted to drink. Since I decided that she would order the pizza, I had her practice with me several times. When she was ready, I let her order. Initially, she asked for one medium sausage and cheese pizza and two medium sodas, but at the last minute she changed the drink order from two medium sodas to two small sodas. With a very serious face, she explained that she changed our order because she might need extra money at the circus. Not bad thinking for a six-year-old child!

The only part of our order I influenced was to request

take-out. I knew I had to get Abigail to the circus before she popped with excitement. At first, I think she was a bit disappointed that we wouldn't be eating at the restaurant, but I explained that when we got to the fairgrounds where the circus was being held, we would have a picnic. With that new information, she was absolutely giddy!

Abigail wanted to start eating the pizza in the car and I must admit the smell was tempting, but I wanted her to learn a bit about manners and patience, plus, I was having fun watching her anticipate the event. We managed to get a good parking space since we were so early. Then we were able to find a perfect little grassy area with a lone tree by the arena. I let Abigail have the honors of setting up our picnic area and opening the pizza box. When she opened the box, her expression was as excited as if she were opening a long-lost treasure chest. We had plastic forks, but I told her since we were on a picnic, we could just use our hands to eat. That added even more excitement to her eyes. She wanted to serve the pizza, so I gave her the (dull) plastic knife to separate the pieces. I explained that the server must always give everyone else their pieces before she served herself. She agreed but muttered that she was glad I was the only other person because she was ready to eat.

Enough anticipation; it was time to eat! I ate two pieces and Abigail ate the remaining four. She didn't gobble them down. Instead, she seemed to savor every bite and scrambled after the little sausage chunks that fell off her piece and then popped them into her mouth. I knew if I let her, she would lick the cardboard box, but she managed to clean it off well enough with her fingers. To me, my two pieces were just average tasting, but I could tell just by watching Abigail that the pizza was a real treat for her.

At five fifteen we collected our things and went to find our seats inside the arena. This particular arena was well documented in architectural books for its unique design. It was special because of its immense size and the fact that there were no inner supports to obstruct anyone's view. Due to its size and the popularity of the Barnum and Bailey circus, the place was going to be filled to capacity. Wanting to make sure Abigail didn't miss anything, we discussed all the sights, sounds, and smells we were experiencing as we entered the outer area of the arena.

Because of the difficulty she and I were having getting through the huge crowd of people in that outer area, I decided to ask Abigail if she wanted anything to eat or drink or if she needed to use the restroom before we went to our seats. I got an affirmative answer for each question. First, the restroom! We made our way downstairs to the enormous bathroom, and we were so surprised to see what seemed to be an endless line! The suggestion to visit the ladies' room seemed to remind Abigail how much she needed to use the restroom so she hopped up and down wriggling in great discomfort until it was her turn. After we emptied our bladders and washed our hands, we were ready to eat again.

Though I had some back-up money in case we needed it, I reminded Abigail there was a limit to my money. After she practiced again, she ordered for both of us. Still wanting to stretch her money, she asked for a small bag of popcorn and a small Coke for each of us. This time, her rationale was that she wanted to use her leftover money so she could buy one of the programs she had caught a glimpse of as we were walking around. I was pleased that she grasped the concept that my money had a limit, but I needed to use my back-up money to get the program. There was no way I would have said no to getting her that colorful program with the large photos of elephants in the centerfold!

With our popcorn, drinks, and program in hand, we set off to find our seats. As we walked through the large doors that led into the actual arena, Abigail gasped with an exuberant "WOW!" Her mouth dropped open, and her eyes were like saucers. The actual arena was huge. Then add all the bright lights, bold colors, the multitude of people, and the myriad commotions the circus brings and it really was a "WOW!"

We were having trouble finding our seats so we asked an usher to help us. Abigail was so sweet asking the man for help and thanking him very politely after he walked us to the correct seats. For being so young, I was impressed with her friendly manners.

The actual circus performances are a blur to me. I watched Abigail more than the show and for that I had a front row seat. She gave belly laughs when the clowns performed, practically stopped breathing when the lions came out, giggled uncontrollably with the trick dogs, and sat in awe of the enormous elephants. Other than the clowns, the people performing their acts didn't seem to impress her much. She just loved the animals! Maybe in her mind she sees people every day, but animals were a novelty.

When the circus was over, we sat and watched most of the people leave so we didn't have to fight the crowds. Then we walked down to the area where the circus crew was working with the animals and were treated to another elephant show. Abigail started screaming with laughter when she saw an elephant lift its tail and go to the bathroom. She couldn't get over the sound or the amount! Abigail sure pitied the crewman who followed behind the elephant and had to clean up the messes it made. The elephant's bathroom skills were the topic of her conversation all the way to the pay phone in the front lobby of the arena. For all I knew, she may have still been mumbling about them when I was talking to Mr. Hales.

Mr. Hales told me to meet him at eight at the local gas station near Abigail's home, and he would be in his van waiting for us. Sure enough, he was there waiting. Before we left, I got permission from the gas station attendant to leave my car in his lot for about fifteen minutes. Then, Abigail and I got into the van, buckled up our seatbelts, and headed to her neighborhood.

I know I am rather naive about some situations, but I was raw green when it came to what I was going to see. At that time in my life, I never knew how different neighborhoods could be, let alone the fact that they could be separated by just a few streets.

As we drove into the apartment complex, Mr. Hales' unknown van drew a great deal of attention. There were many teenagers and young adults hanging around the parking lot. Many were draped over cars with their boom boxes blaring. Most of them stopped what they were doing and stared us down as we drove by them. While Mr. Hales was driving, he muttered under his breath that he knew that I shouldn't have come and that he had made a mistake letting me. A few of the teenagers followed our van until it stopped. I probably should have been afraid or at least a bit nervous, but I was neither. I was too busy being heartbroken as I watched my sweet, adorable, well-mannered, little Abigail transform into someone else. Her speech was the first thing to change. She was harsh and abrasive to Mr. Hales and me. She snapped at me and barked at Mr. Hales to stop by her section of apartments. We could have driven closer, but she demanded that he stop immediately!

As soon as the van stopped, Abigail flipped off her seatbelt, jerked open the door, and jumped out. I hurriedly followed behind her, telling Mr. Hales I was going with her but that wasn't going to happen without him going with me. He now ordered me to wait for him. As I stood outside of the van, I quickly saw how out of place I was and that I truly needed to wait for Mr. Hales. Abigail hustled ahead of us, and I was crushed as I watched her dainty girlish walk change to a hard militant strut the closer she got to her apartment building.

The teenagers were running behind us taunting me about my skin color, my clothes, and my *kind*. One boy kicked a soccer ball and hit me in the hip. I just kept walking, but Mr. Hales scolded the boy and shooed them all off. About ten yards from her apartment door, Abigail started running. Mr. Hales held my arm to make me stop and said that we would wait there.

I watched my darling girl bang on the rickety door. There were lights on inside of the apartment, but no one came for quite a while. Finally, the door opened but the screen door was still shut. The woman who appeared was swearing at Abigail, and Abigail was swearing right back at her! If this scene wasn't bad enough, the screen door couldn't hide the fact that the woman was naked! Evidently, Abigail disrupted *something* and the woman wasn't too happy about it. I was horrified at what Abigail had to go back to and horrified at what she had to become in order to survive.

Abigail never turned around to acknowledge us, and I didn't expect her to. I wish I could say I was glad to know she was home safely, but all I could say was that she was home. As we went back to the van, the boys started taunting me again while Mr. Hales tried to explain what happened. I might have been raw green, but I wasn't stupid. I knew. I also knew I hated it.

Mr. Hales took me to my car. I thanked him for saving me from my stupidity. He just laughed and thanked me for all I was doing for Abigail because he knew that she sure needed me. Driving home that night, I couldn't get Abigail out of my mind. I knew I couldn't help her outside of school, but I certainly could make a difference in school. I would work even harder to make that part of Abigail's life more loving, supportive, and consistent than ever.

Olivia

OLIVIA WAS ONLY eleven but she loved to mother. She made sure everyone was taken care of and happy. Now it was time that someone took care of her. Olivia started the year out as a new student in my class. She was eager to learn, hard-working, and very polite, all the signs of being raised by a grandmother. And that was exactly who was raising her. The grandmother was also the person I needed to talk with about getting Olivia's placement changed.

Even though Olivia was great to have in class, she needed more help than my program could offer. As a fourth grader, she was functioning on a first to second grade level across the board. Not only that, she had extreme difficulty changing gears when coming and going from my class to her regular fourth grade class. The whole routine was disruptive, ineffective, and unfair to her. I knew it and so did her regular classroom teacher, her grand-mother, and the school-based committee. After I completed all the required and detailed observations of her in both classes, we, meaning the classroom teacher, grandmother, school-based committee, and I, agreed that a self-contained classroom setting was the appropriate placement to meet Olivia's needs. These decisions were never made in haste or taken lightly, and since this type of change was an especially major one, all checks and balances were reviewed by each party involved.

Testing showed that, indeed, Olivia's difficulties were all-encompassing and not just in one or two areas as with a learning-disabled child. That meant even the disability title had to be changed. Instead of being labeled learning disabled, it would need to be changed to educable mentally retarded, EMR. (Remember, this label has changed, but at the time I was teaching, this was the official term.) I hated the label EMR, but all of Olivia's test results and observations consistently showed that she needed help in all areas of academics along with many age appropriate life skills. Due to the extremely low scores on all of her tests, not only did she qualify as EMR, but the results gave unquestionable evidence supporting self-contained placement. This placement would offer Olivia the opportunity to have the consistency of staying in the same class all day long with one specially trained teacher and one teacher's assistant with no more than nine other students. I may have hated the term, but I knew this placement would offer her the educational instruction and environment Olivia desperately needed. It took several months to collect all the data on Olivia and hold all the conferences with the necessary parties. When I had all the information gathered, I wrote up my findings in quadruplicate and sent my recommendation to the Central Office.

Weeks went by and I finally received a response from the Central Office Placement Committee. To my astonishment, my well-documented referral for self-contained placement was denied! Not only was the teaching situation denied, so was the change of Olivia's category. There was no reason given; my request was just denied. Not only did the placement committee deny both of my requests, they had the audacity to tell me to change my recommendation for Olivia to reflect an upgrade of LD resource. This meant that she would stay in my room the maximum amount of time, which was three hours.

She was already with me for that amount of time and it wasn't working!

School was long over, and it was getting dark outside. Though I tried to do other work in my room to get ready for the next day, I kept rereading that letter in total disbelief. I couldn't believe that Olivia's recommended placement had been denied but more than that, I was shocked that this high-officiating Master and Doctorate degree-filled team of people told me to change my recommendation! The unprofessional request made by these people was jaw dropping.

My mom was in the neighborhood near my school that evening, and she stopped by the trailer on the good chance I was working late. It was more normal for me to be there late than not be there. Fortunately for Olivia and me, Mom came by to visit. As soon as she said hello to me, I started ranting and raving about the letter I had received and the situation with Olivia. I handed her a letter that I had started as a response and asked her opinion. My mom is awesome when it comes to situations like this. She bluntly told me that my letter was far too weak, and I should write exactly what I had just told her. She cheered me on saying that if I believed my recommendation was accurate, I should stand up to the committee and hold firm to my recommendation.

My final response to the Central Office Placement Committee was not as strong as my mom probably would have liked, but what I did write shook up the committee. In my letter, I outlined what procedures I had followed and how the decision was made for EMR self-contained placement. The final part of the letter stated that this was the only appropriate placement for Olivia, and my recommendation would stay as is.

When this committee received my letter, I guess it rattled them all. One of the Central Office supervisors called to let me know that I had been requested to attend the next placement meeting to explain my letter. She haughtily stated that in all her years, no teacher had ever been asked to come to the committee meeting. Personally, I thought that fact should be an embarrassing admission since teachers' input should be a vital part of the placement process. After all, we were the ones who knew the students the best. For the moment though, I kept my thoughts to myself and simply thanked the woman for the invitation.

Because of the type of students I worked with and the way I ran my class, finding a substitute was always difficult. Fortunately, the morning I had to go to the Central Office for this inquisition, my favorite substitute was available so I didn't have to worry too much about my students while I was gone. I knew she and Mrs. Martin would handle everything quite well.

The woman who called to invite me to the meeting said that it would last about half an hour, maybe less, so I believed I would be back to school without missing too much. I never liked missing any part of my school day, but knowing I wouldn't be gone long and that my students were going to be in good hands with two very capable people, I didn't worry.

I dressed in a professional outfit and had all my documentation organized to plead my case. I might have been able to fool everyone around me, but I was terrified. I didn't like any kind of confrontation let alone confronting people who held my employment in their hands. Knowing those same people were not very happy with me didn't help matters. I believed they weren't happy with me, even though I had never met any of them, because people don't usually react too kindly to someone making life harder for them. I laughed quietly to myself when I realized I wasn't too happy with them either!

With my nerves all over the board—nervous, worried, angry, scared, and intimidated, I knew I had to ignore my negative preconception toward these people. I also had to muster up as much confidence, kindness, and professionalism as I could when I talked with this group of people. They held the future for Olivia and me in their hands. I knew I was right with this placement issue. Olivia deserved to be in a class that was appropriate for her. I created this belief as a mental mantra to help bolster my confidence as I entered the Central Office building.

Before I opened the door to the conference room, I just stood there trying to give myself a pep talk and calm down. I felt everyone could see my heart pounding under my blouse. When I opened the door, I saw seven people all seated around a large conference table. No one rose to greet me. Basically, they just stared in my direction. One daring soul spoke and said he trusted I was Miss Chandler. I responded with a warm and pleasant smile followed with a nod. As I was sitting down, I thanked them all for inviting me to the meeting. I told them that I realized how very busy they were and appreciated the time they were giving me. I was going to say more, but I was interrupted by a rude and domineering woman in her forties. She said they all had read my letter, and she could speak for everyone present. She said that they were not used to receiving letters like mine, let alone with the tone in which it was written. She stopped and looked at me as if she wanted me to apologize or beg for forgiveness. So much for the pep talk I gave myself to stay kind or even nice to these people. I responded with an enthusiastic, albeit nervous and a bit aggravated tone by saying that I was not used to having my well-documented, well-researched recommendation being rejected either so I guessed that was why we were meeting!

Though I rarely spoke in this harsh tone, I knew I wanted what was best for Olivia and that I had to stand up for her. I saw Olivia and my other students as my own and that feeling brought out an assertive personality I didn't know I had. I was scared to death on the inside, but I had learned to be a good actress. I held onto this brave façade throughout the entire meeting, which lasted one and a half hours!

As with all the conferences and meetings I had with the parents of my students, I asked the placement committee to state their concerns first. They questioned many issues that had already been answered in my documentation. The more they talked, the more it was obvious they had either not read any of the paperwork I had sent, or they had just spot-read it.

Finally, it was my turn to respond to all of their comments. Just by listening to what they had said, I knew what the problem was. I wanted to make them say it but no one had the guts. So, I said it for them. Their problem with the situation was that she was black! As soon as I said it, they all may have had different facial expressions, but they showed the same emotion of guilt! There was a long uncomfortable silence until one younger man had the nerve to say that the quotas for blacks had been met for the EMR classification for both resource and self-contained classrooms. With a straight face, he said that Olivia couldn't be EMR! I took a moment to bridle my tongue and then retorted by declaring that it was like they were saying they had the quotas filled for blacks so she couldn't be black. I despised quotas and this was a perfect example of why. Children, and people for that matter, don't ever fit neatly in quotas.

Mentally, I started pushing up my sleeves to fight. My Olivia wasn't going to be pushed into a class situation in order to make government paperwork look good. I know this is why the meeting lasted so long. I started from scratch and explained what a day was like for Olivia. They had to realize what they were asking of this human being. This beautiful girl was going to have to suffer because of numbers on a piece of paper that were dictated by people who had no regard for her as a person. It just wasn't right! I drew a picture of what Olivia's day would be like with the correct placement in a self-contained class, the continuity of her day, and the advances that she could make, unlike what was happening with her resource placement, where she was learning nothing because she was lost academically and socially and was having difficulties switching back and forth from her regular classroom to my room. She deserved better!

I brought in the human side of Olivia's situation. I explained how Olivia gave all she could to learn and willingly worked hard but to no avail. She regularly shed tears because she couldn't get herself on track in my class after having come from her regular class. These were daily struggles. Disruptions were painfully distracting to her. Even if she were to stay in my room the maximum number of hours, that left three and a half hours where she would be totally lost with what was being taught in the regular classroom. I explained that this was a little girl whose future was very dismal due to their decision. I summed it up by imploring them to understand her side of the story. If they understood her story, surely they would know she needed their help to receive a positive learning environment and they would place her in an EMR self-contained classroom.

When I was finished, the young man recapped a few things I had said and then thanked me for coming in and telling my side of the issue. He said the team would review the new information and reconsider Olivia's placement. Nothing he or anyone else said gave me the feeling that anything would change, but I thanked them again for their time and went around and shook hands with each of them. As I left the room, I noticed everyone had the same angry expressions as when I entered, and again they all stayed seated.

When I walked out of the conference room and the door shut behind me, I took my first good breath of air since the meeting began. I was so relieved to have the meeting behind me, but I had no feel for how my information had been received. All I knew then was that time would tell, and I had to hurry back to school.

It took just a week for me to get a response from the committee. The envelope addressed to me was thin; I feared it was not a good sign. With a sick feeling starting to build in my stomach, I opened it. But it was good news—Olivia was approved for placement in an EMR self-contained classroom and would start in one week! Placements like this would normally take months before the student would be moved to a new class. I had to chuckle at the speed of her approval because if it had been anything different, the placement committee must have known I would be back!

Paperwork

I HAVE NEVER been very organized with my paperwork at home or at work. It never caused me any problem until I kicked up some dust and ruffled some feathers concerning the placement for Olivia.

In the school system where I worked, each teacher was usually observed once a year by the principal. The planned observation usually took about an hour and then there would be a fifteen-minute meeting with the principal to go over his report. Signatures would be signed, and then the observation process was over. When there was a concern or a problem with a teacher, he or she was observed by an administrator from the Central Office.

Well, guess what? I was a problem so I was visited not once but several times by the school district's Central Office supervisor. The observations were all unannounced, which was not the norm either, but I really didn't care. Anyone was welcome to visit my class as I had an open-door policy. With the open-door policy, I could never guarantee what the observer would see. There was rarely a normal day in my class. I was okay with that fact, but I also had to be okay with observers and visitors not being okay with the unusual happenings in class. When people did come to observe, I would put them to work if they were there for very long. Since I was always short on help in my room, I never passed up an extra set of hands to assist with my students.

Of all the observers who came into my room, I think the only person who genuinely welcomed the opportunity to give that much-needed helping hand was my favorite principal, Mr. Briggs. He thoroughly enjoyed getting involved with the students in my class and any other class for that matter. Mr. Briggs had a personal policy that if he had to reprimand or punish a student, then soon after the punishment, he would find at least two positive occasions to interact with that same child. Due to several of my students getting into skirmishes on the playground or on the buses, we saw Mr. Briggs a lot. You could tell he loved the children and his job. As for the students, they loved him and had a great deal of respect for him.

When the Central Office supervisor came to observe my class the first time, I tried to get her involved with my students, but she was so put off by them and treated them with such disrespect that on the following visits, I didn't even try to get her to help. It is a sad commentary when a school supervisor does not work well with children!

I could tell that this woman was searching for something with which to hang me. The way she looked at me and the tone she had in her voice was a dead giveaway that she didn't like me, but when she started grilling me about specifics on my students, their needs, and their parents, I knew she was out for blood. Unfortunately for her, everything she asked me I could answer without hesitation. I think that frustrated her. She may have been frustrated for a while, but she finally found a problem.

The heinous problem that she seemed delighted to have uncovered was my lack of organizational habits with my desk and filing system. My classroom and my students' work were always in excellent order but as for my own paperwork, well, that was just not important to me. I had everything, and I could find everything, but it was all in one big pile, and I mean *big* pile, on my desk. I never sat at my desk so I just piled all my paperwork on top of it as the paperwork came in.

My students would tease me about my desk. One student even took a picture of it to hold as "blackmail" if I ever tried to make him clean his desk. The funny thing was that I never got after my students about their desks. I would show them ways to be organized, and the kids would either choose to be organized or not. I learned that as the student found the need to be organized, he or she would decide to become organized. I believe so many teachers and students lose their sanity over the war of organization. I figured as long as the students could find what they wanted with little time lost and they were happy, then why create a problem. I have seen more damage done to students by teachers demanding neatness and trying to make them do something they weren't ready for than I have for students having messy desks.

I understand this because when it came to paperwork, I always had trouble being neat. I rarely lost things, and I could find what I needed within a reasonable amount of time. I was happy and comfortable with my organizational system. That is all that should matter. Or so I thought! Well, not according to this supervisor. Now that she had some dirt on me, she wrote up her report. The only negative issue she had to say about me was concerning my filing system and did she ever blow that out of proportion. Fortunately for me, I had Mr. Briggs's support during this inquisition.

One afternoon, Mrs. McKay called me to the principal's office to go over this formal report with the Central Office supervisor and Mr. Briggs. I was not happy at all when I heard what was in the report, but I wasn't surprised. Sadly, I had no leg to stand on because I wasn't neat with my paperwork. What upset me was that the issue was written with such a negative slant that it made me sound like a poor teacher.

There was really nothing for me to say, but Mr. Briggs had a lot to say, and he didn't hold back. I was so impressed with how he stood up for me. Obviously irritated at this woman, he promised her that he would not stand by and have her report go into my permanent file when it was so petty. He clarified that I had an excellent record of performance and for this issue to be blown out of proportion was inexcusable. Mr. Briggs promised her that he would go straight to the superintendent to fight the issue if need be.

For me, it was worth going through all of this to hear what Mr. Briggs thought about me. I had grown accustomed to being treated as the necessary annoyance by my first principal, so it was refreshing to hear such positive comments. Mr. Briggs continued talking with this woman by pointing out the outrageous student load of cross categorical students that I was being expected to teach with no teaching assistant and little money for supplies. Then he went on with all the student successes I had achieved and that was what I was being paid for, not to sit behind a desk and fill out forms to justify her job. He elaborated that he had even more respect for me as a teacher because with my workload, it was obvious to him that I had my priorities straight.

Mr. Briggs continued drilling her by asking if I had been delinquent with any of my work to her or anyone else at the Central Office. She stiffly replied that I was current with all my reports and other requirements. He continued by asking if all of my work had been filled out properly and fully. She barely eked out a "Yes."

From this point on, I don't know what happened. Mr. Briggs turned to me and very kindly said I was excused and that I could return to my classroom. As I stood up, he assured me that everything was going to be all right and for me not to worry about the report anymore. From that moment on, the issues of my organizational skills or this report were never brought up again, and I never worried about it. What did surprise me was from that fateful day forward, the Central Office supervisor was always very kind and courteous to me, which wasn't normal. I would have loved to have been a fly on the wall that afternoon after Mr. Briggs had excused me so I could hear what else was said, but truly, I had heard all I needed. Whether the child-adverse school supervisor liked me or not didn't matter. I knew I had the respect and support of someone who truly loved kids maybe even more than I did!

Devon

THE FIRST DAY of each new school year was always quite nerve wracking for both my students and me. This year, my fourth full year, was no different. Many of my returning students just dropped by my room to say hello, but my new students would arrive at their scheduled times a little unsure of what to expect.

Devon, one of my new students, came in very differently though. He walked into my room with an overly compensating strut of fake confidence and displayed a dramatic frown. Looking at this very unhappy child, I was taken by surprise to see how his left eye wandered any which way and it never seemed to keep up with his right eye. I was puzzled since there was no mention of an eye problem in his confidential file. I knew I would have to look into this situation, but that would have to be at a later time. At that moment, I wanted to start off on the right foot with Devon.

Since Devon was new, I wanted to ask a few basic questions to begin to get to know him, but all my attempts were met with him looking at me and turning away in a disgusted manner. He never uttered a word. So I ignored him. As a matter of fact, I didn't even look at him the entire hour he was scheduled to be in my room. I wasn't trying to be mean; I just wanted to give him some space and time to get adjusted to the room and me. I was certain he had been reprimanded all too many times for his seemingly rude behavior, and I didn't want to be yet another bothersome teacher. I went on talking with the other new and returning students. I knew Devon could learn about our room and the rules by overhearing my conversations with the other students.

When it was time for him to leave, I just called out the three names of the students who were scheduled to go back to their regular classroom. Devon was one of them. The other two students were ones I had had in previous years so they were used to coming up to give and get a hug and say their goodbyes. I paid Devon no special attention, and he just left the room.

It was quite touching to see how the other students remaining in the room reacted to me ignoring Devon. They questioned why I was so mean to the new boy, and they all stuck up for him saying that I didn't make him feel welcome. I quickly clarified that I was not being mean. I explained that it was obvious that Devon didn't want to be talked *to* and he wasn't ready to be talked *with* and I respected that. I was just going to give him time. By the looks on their faces, I am not sure they understood so I encouraged them to be as nice to Devon as they always were to new students. Devon's issue was with adults, not them.

To my surprise, Devon started talking the next day. During class, Richard and I were joking around and having a wonderful time and I could tell that Devon was watching us. Richard, in his usual charismatic manner, told some jokes and riddles. With one riddle, he asked me for an answer. I can't remember what it was, but my response didn't suit Richard or Devon. The two boys started laughing and laughing. Devon, still laughing, said he couldn't believe I didn't know the answer. He replied the answer was *such 'n such* and started laughing even harder.

That was all it took for us to start up a dialogue. I asked him if he knew a joke or riddle he could share with us. He shook his head complaining that all he knew were lame jokes but with friendly prodding from a few other students, Devon gave it a try anyway. Unfortunately, he was right. His jokes were quite weak, but that didn't stop the other students, Devon, or me from cracking up over each one he told. We even got to a point where we just laughed at whatever was said. Thanks to Richard and my other students, Devon and I got off on the right foot very quickly. We had a long way to go before Devon would pull down the wall he had built around himself, but over time, I had the joy of getting to know what a sweet boy Devon really was.

Even though we hit it off quickly, there were still many months where it was obvious that Devon was just an angry boy. He obviously internalized a great deal of negative emotion, but I was not sure what it was about. This was exceptionally sad because he was just a second grader! Most days he came strutting into my class with a bad-ass attitude. He didn't have a chip on his shoulder—he had a 2 x 4 on his shoulder! Sometimes, it seemed he was saying with his body language that if you looked at him wrong or said something he didn't like, you were in trouble.

Keep in mind, this child was only eight years old. Physically, he looked so much older. His skin was all marked up from scabs to scars leaving only guesses as to what had happened to him. His lower lip protruded and was also heavily scarred. His eyes, more than anything else, bewildered me. I depended so much on *seeing* children through their eyes and with Devon, the severely lazy eye was so distracting. I had to teach myself to study the right eye and not get thrown off by the left.

On a day that he and I had some one-on-one time and feeling I had a fairly good rapport with him, I asked Devon about his eye. He responded with such willingness it seemed he had been waiting for someone to talk with him about his eye. He explained how he suffered with headaches and other physical discomforts from his eye. He also explained, in his eight-year old way, how embarrassed he was because of how odd he looked and how hard it was to hear the ridicule from so many other students in his regular classroom.

Another day while talking with Devon, I asked him again about his eye. He just shrugged his shoulders and replied, "What is there to know?" I asked yes or no questions like "Does your eye bother you?" and "Can you see out of it?" Unfortunately, all I got were "Nah's." I changed my questioning to ask what the doctor had said about his eye. Assuming that Devon had been to a doctor just showed how naïve I was. He admitted that he had never seen an eye doctor let alone seen one specifically about his lazy eye. I worked very hard to cover up my shock at this information. With such an obvious issue with his eye and to hear that he had never been to an eye doctor was unbelievable. I am sure there were many other reasons why Devon was angry and tough, but I am also sure his eye didn't help matters.

Later that afternoon, I scoured through his confidential and regular files and couldn't find anything regarding his eye. Sometimes paperwork was slow to get to me, and I could tell there were some forms that I didn't have in my files so I went to talk to the school counselor. Unfortunately, she was at another school that afternoon, so I decided, against my better judgment, to talk with his regular classroom teacher. There were very few people I didn't like at the school, but Mrs. Cranston ranked as one of my three least favorites at this school. I didn't want to wait until the next day to talk with the counselor and though I may not have liked Mrs. Cranston, I thought she might have different information on Devon than I had, so I went to talk with her.

Mrs. Cranston was the type of teacher who taught smart kids well. They made her look good, and her job was so much easier. She didn't like any student who didn't learn with ease, who didn't adore her, or who was not a pretty person. In her mind, Devon missed on all three counts. When I questioned her about Devon, she retorted, "Ah, so you've met my escapee!" Devon had another strike against him; she expected him to be trouble. I avoided a confrontation, for the moment, because I wanted some information. My efforts were useless because she had no interest in helping me. All she could talk about was how perfect her class would be if Devon wasn't in it. She even admitted she had tried to have him removed from her class and couldn't believe that the principal refused her request. Getting nowhere with her, I excused myself and realized I had to wait until the next day to talk with the counselor.

Bright and early the next morning, I landed at the counselor's door. I told her all about my concern with Devon's eye and asked if I could look through the confidential files she had on him. Every school needs a counselor like Ms. Thomas. She always went beyond the call of duty to help the teachers and the students, and amazingly, she did it with great enthusiasm and ease. For the next hour, the two of us poured through numerous papers. His file was thick with all kinds of reports about his poor behavior, but nothing substantial was written about his eye. One examiner did write that Devon could read more accurately with his right eye than his left using the 'E' chart, but that was all. We checked his regular file that was in the office and there was nothing except more information about how difficult Devon was in class. I just couldn't understand how such an obvious physical issue could be overlooked. Even with all the numerous tests he had to undergo to get into my program, no evaluator had ever written that he could have a vision problem!

I was consumed with angry thoughts about the school system's oversight, but then I also harbored anger toward his mother. She absolutely should have done something for Devon. It really wasn't up to the school. I had plenty of parents who had no education to speak of, but they took good care of their children. I knew it didn't take any education to know that something was wrong or at least something was unusual about Devon's eye and that it should be looked into. There were clinics that did not charge for people who couldn't pay. The bottom line to all of this mess was that there was no excuse for Devon suffering all these years with his vision problem.

I called some ophthalmologists as well as a friend, who was an optometrist. They all said the same thing; Devon should get his eyes checked immediately because there was a strong chance that his eye would get worse, or he could even lose the sight in his left eye if it was the condition they all suspected it was.

The mother made many excuses why she couldn't take Devon to the clinic, but I became such a nuisance she finally took him to the doctor, probably so I would leave her alone. I didn't care why she took Devon, I was just glad he got there. Sure enough, there was a vision problem. Surprise! Surprise! The rest of the information made me sick when I heard it. At this time, Devon's eye condition was irreversible, and there was a great possibility he would lose his sight in that eye. What was so frustrating was that this condition could have been corrected if he had been properly diagnosed earlier.

Growing up, I was always told that life wasn't fair and there were no guarantees, but it really wasn't fair that this child had to suffer because of neglect by both his mother and by the school system. For me, it was so frustrating because it was now too late for anyone to help him.

One good thing that came from all this was that I learned this disorder was genetic and usually ran in the family. With that information, I went straight to Devon's little brother's kindergarten teacher, Mrs. Millner. This woman happened to be a very dear friend of mine, and she was also the epitome of a great teacher. She challenged herself to learn more, was exceptionally creative, and always went beyond what was expected of her position to do the best job she could for her students as well as for her fellow teachers.

With the information I gave Mrs. Millner, she went to the mother, explaining the seriousness of this medical issue now with her other son. She successfully convinced the mother to have Joehna tested. Sure enough, he had the same disorder that Devon had and underwent treatment and therapy to correct his problem. The doctor reported that Joehna's eye would probably be totally corrected since it was caught so early.

One of the biggest lessons I *never* learned as a teacher was to realize I had limitations and to accept the fact that I couldn't fix all the problems my students had. In the situation with Devon, I may not have been able to help him with his vision, but I knew Mrs. Millner and I were a big part of helping his little brother avoid the same fate. Though I was thrilled for Joehna, I still ached for Devon and felt so sad that I couldn't help him with his vision.

The Bandana

AS I MENTIONED earlier, Mrs. Cranston was one of my least favorite people at the school. She certainly didn't have good feelings toward me either but for different reasons. I don't believe she had any real feelings about me one way or another but rather she didn't like what I represented. If she had to work with me that meant she had a difficult student in her class.

In addition to not respecting her as a teacher, I found that Mrs. Cranston was also the most difficult to work with in regard to scheduling her students to come to my room. Actually, I should say she was the easiest because she would not budge with her schedule at all and that was final. Easy! No surprises. In her mind, I am sure she already felt she was being inconvenienced enough as it was to have a problem child in her class at all. Her interactions with any of my students placed in her room never showed any concern or compassion. Instead, those interactions just revealed annoyance!

She told me time and time again that she was responsible for the child, and I would have to work around her schedule. Now this didn't mean that if one of my students got out of hand while in her classroom that she would deal with him or her. Oh no! That child would land on my doorstep any time of the day with no regard for my schedule or the child she was sending. By no means was Mrs. Cranston the only teacher who sent students at any time, but she definitely sent them more often than any other teacher.

I didn't make an issue when she or other regular classroom teachers would just send my students any time to my room because I felt it would get back to the student and these children already felt like outcasts. I did ask the teachers not to let the students finagle their way to my room, but if a teacher sent them, no matter why or when they came to my room, I would genuinely welcome them and tell them how glad I was that they were there.

Because of Mrs. Cranston's contempt for Devon, some days he would be in my room all day because she plainly and simply didn't want to have him in her room. She would always tell me the work was over Devon's head, but that was far from the truth since Devon was a very bright student. There was nothing wrong with his academics except for falling behind a little due to his behavior. His behavior was the only reason he was in my room. In Mrs. Cranston's opinion, anyone in my class was dumb, hopeless, and not worth wasting her precious time.

Over the few years I had been working at this school, I just tolerated her and her behavior toward my students and me until things erupted over Devon. There was a PTA meeting coming up in a month and a small number of students from each grade were going to perform dance routines for that meeting. The P.E. teacher, Mrs. Moore, had created a wonderful routine for the students using country music. She was working with all the students, even though just a handful of them would be chosen to actually perform at the PTA meeting. It was fun to see how intently the students reacted to the dance practices since they had to compete for a place on the performing team.

The dance practices were for all the students, and they were held every day. Devon loved the practices and couldn't wait to get to P.E. class. That is until one day when he made a 180 degree turn with his feelings, and I couldn't get him out of the room to go to practice. He moaned and groaned making all types of excuses for not wanting to go. Two big excuses he used were that he really didn't like the dance and the performance was a stupid thing to be doing anyway. I knew that none of what he was saying was true, especially since I knew he had made the final cut.

With a great deal of cajoling, I managed to get Devon to tell me what was wrong. According to him, Mrs. Cranston had made the decision that he would not be in the performance. She told him since his work wasn't up to par (which wasn't true), he'd have to stay in my room during P.E. until after the performance, therefore, he would not have to practice anymore. Her reasoning didn't make sense since all the students were required to practice regardless of whether they performed or not.

I gave Devon a big hug and said there must be a mistake. He was truly one of the best dancers out of all of the students and deserved to be in the performance! He not only loved to dance, he had the rhythm and the steps down perfectly. After I told him there must have been a mistake, he looked at me like I was crazy. It was Mrs. Cranston who was mistaken if she thought she was going to keep Devon out of the performance.

At the end of the day, after all the students had been dismissed, I went to see Mrs. Cranston. I politely stated my concern for Devon's distraught behavior and asked if she might know anything that might have spurred this unusual behavior. She said she didn't. I truly believed her. I don't think she had enough compassion to understand what she had done to Devon. I continued by describing how excited Devon had been about being in the performance. She nonchalantly clarified that he was not allowed to participate due to his grades.

I knew his grades were not that bad, but I used her excuse against her. I asked how many other students she was keeping out due to their grades. Before she knew what I was up to, she said that no one else was being held out.

Mrs. Cranston struggled to get herself out of the hole she had dug by saying that she just didn't want him in the performance. I repeated her words and then added that she didn't want him in the performance because he didn't look the part. She smiled and agreed, as if I actually saw her point. Foolish woman!

I made sure she knew that under no circumstance would I stand by while she crushed a child's spirit because he didn't fit into her pretty little world! She was shocked by my comment and even tried to convince me why she was right. She explained that he would be laughed at and made a fool. Ha! Now this woman cared about Devon's feelings…not likely. All I said to her was that I was going to guarantee he did perform because he was without question one of the best dancers and deserved to be there. Since we were at a stalemate, it was time for me to leave.

As I passed the office, I was thrilled to see the principal and Mrs. Moore talking. They were actually working out details for the PTA meeting. Having them both right there, I quickly inquired about the rumor I'd heard concerning Devon not being allowed in the program. Neither knew anything about this rumor and asked where I'd heard it. I brushed off their question by saying that it didn't really matter; I just wanted to make sure Devon was allowed to perform since he had made the final cut. They both, simultaneously, assured me that he would be in the program.

Mrs. Moore bragged about how good Devon was and divulged that she had already decided to put him in the front row. Incredible! Devon would be so thrilled to hear the news. Mrs. Cranston would be mortified. After I left the office, Mrs. Moore ran to catch up with me so she could ask whether it was Mrs. Cranston claiming that Devon was not going to be in the program. Before I could even respond, and I am not sure what I would have said, Mrs. Moore admitted she was worried Mrs. Cranston might cause a problem for Devon. Without knowing what I had already said to Mrs. Cranston, Mrs. Moore vowed that she would not let Mrs. Cranston crush Devon's spirit by forbidding him to be in the performance. She repeated several times that Devon was one of her best students and that he had earned the right to be in the program. In parting, I asked Mrs. Moore to tell Devon the good news because he was so convinced that he would not be in the program that it would take hearing it from her, the program director, before he would believe it.

The next day, when Devon came into my room, I told him that Mrs. Moore wanted to see him before he started his work with me. He was still depressed and said he already knew he wasn't going to be in the performance so he didn't need to see her. Almost having to threaten a punishment, I finally convinced him to leave.

When he returned from seeing Mrs. Moore, Devon was a transformed child. He bounced into my room and claimed that I would never, NEVER be able to guess his good news! He was jumping up and down giggling as only Devon could, saying, "Guess, guess!" He walked around the room showing his manly strut as I stuttered out a few guesses. He landed himself right in front of my face and said, "You aren't even close!" I begged him to tell me because I was so excited.

He proudly announced that he was going to be in the second grade dance performance at the PTA program! Mrs. Moore was even going to get him an outfit to wear for the show. He added, with precious enthusiasm, that he was also going to wear a bandana! He wasn't at all sure what a bandana was but it sounded cool. Then he explained that Mrs. Moore had made him the leader of the dance because she said he was the best dancer! Under his breath he said, "I am the best! I am the best!"..., savoring the moment. He was just adorable!

Mrs. Moore assured Devon that Mrs. Cranston was totally in favor of him performing and apologized for the miscommunication with his teacher. Though Mrs. Moore might have given a fabricated and more than gracious explanation about Mrs. Cranston's comments, all that really mattered was that Devon was excited, and now he could start enjoying his success.

Unfortunately for me, there was a scheduling conflict the night of the performance. I was taking a computer class at a nearby college, and my class met on the same night as the PTA performance. I was not one to miss class, and this night would be no exception, but I decided I would be a bit late since I had to see Devon perform.

Thankfully, the second graders were third to perform and when it was their turn, Mrs. Moore introduced the group and announced that Devon would lead the dancers onto the stage. Right on cue, he proudly stood up and walked to the stage, beaming ear to ear with the rest of his classmates following him. When all the dancers were in place on stage, Devon nodded to Mrs. Moore to begin the music. Since he was the leader, he had to listen for the right measure and beat to begin dancing, which he nailed, and the other dancers followed right in step with him.

The routine Mrs. Moore created was age appropriate for the students, and they were well versed with their steps, so the audience couldn't help but smile and enjoy watching the performance. Personally, I couldn't keep my eyes off of Devon. Mrs. Moore had managed to round up some cowboy-looking clothes that fit Devon. She also was good for her word, and she had bought a blue bandana for him to wear around his neck. He was precious looking in his outfit, and he knew he looked handsome. As for his dancing, he was spectacular. He never missed a step, smiled at the audience, and was enjoying himself immensely. He was having the time of his life!

Already very late for my class, I had to leave as soon as Devon's performance was over. Though I had let Devon know I would have to leave after his performance, I still felt empty not being able to let him know how proud I was of him that night. Fortunately, I knew Mrs. Moore would give Devon plenty of compliments and warm fuzzies. My compliments would have to wait until the next day.

All morning long, I was anxious for Devon to come to class so I could hear his version of the event as well as give him my accolades. At Devon's scheduled time, he strolled into class bearing his memento of the evening. Around his neck was the blue bandana. Recounting the whole evening from the very beginning so all his classmates could hear what happened, Devon seemed to be enjoying himself just as much as he had the night before. At the end of his story, he added that Mrs. Moore had given him the bandana to keep. She explained that he had earned it, and she was extremely proud of him for the excellent job he had done. I reiterated the compliment and gave him a big hug.

Devon tilted his head, his crooked eyes looking my direction, and loudly announced, "Mrs. Cranston doesn't like me." Then he paused and followed that with a confident proclamation, "and I don't care!" He laughed and laughed with this admission. The whole time he was laughing, he was twirling the bandana around his neck. Then he looked directly at me. His eyes were as straight as I had ever seen them and while he held onto his memento he said, "I have the bandana. *SHE* doesn't!" Now this was a very wise and perceptive child. Whether he knew it or not, he was learning a wonderful lesson about rising above people like Mrs. Cranston.

Over the next week, Devon wore the bandana around his neck. I don't think he ever took it off because it got dirtier and grimier as the week went on. After that week though, he did manage to remove it from around his neck but it was always close by—in his pocket, in his book bag, in his hand. Who could blame him for holding it so dearly since it was his trophy of success?

Mr. Dinsmoor

THERE WAS NO such thing as a regular parent/teacher conference for me, but I thought this one was going to be a pleasant and relatively quick meeting. Most of my conferences with parents lasted about an hour though a handful would last a little longer. The way I chose to manage my conferences was very different than the fifteen-minute parent/teacher conferences required by the school. I felt parents shouldn't be rushed. They should be given as much time as they needed to talk and ask questions. After they talked, I had tons of information and strategies to share with them about what was going on in my class and how they could help their child at home. The only thing unusual about this upcoming conference was that it was to be with Derrick Dinsmoor's dad. Usually, dads didn't come to my meetings and most dads usually weren't even around. They were either literally absent or they were too busy at work to get involved with their child. It was nice to see a father interested enough in his child's schoolwork to take time off from work to attend the meeting. I was sorry though that Derrick's mom was not going to join us because she was so kind and incredibly helpful with Derrick at home. For some reason, she was not coming to this meeting.

Mr. Dinsmoor came into my trailer dressed to perfection in a suit and tie. He stood in the doorway and very formally introduced himself. I politely stood and gave him a strong welcoming handshake, stating how glad I was to meet him and how thrilled I was that he had come to the conference. I added, as I said to all the parents I work with, how lucky I was to have his son in my class and how proud he must be of Derrick.

During my conferences, I routinely took five to ten minutes to talk about good things concerning their child. Then I would ask the parent what they were concerned about or what they would like to have happen for their child in regard to working in my program. I found that parents never seemed to have someone to talk to about their problems with their child, so I opened the door for them to express their concerns or even fears.

Like the other parents, Mr. Dinsmoor let it all out. What came out was a surprise. Mr. Dinsmoor, using an authoritative voice that he probably used in boardroom meetings, ordered me to start the proceedings to remove Derrick from my program! I could have named a few of my other students who were close to being released, but Derrick was still having severe problems with certain academic areas. As calmly as I could, I questioned his request by asking what made him feel the need to remove Derrick from my program since he was doing so well. If there was a problem, I would be willing to work things out the best way I could because though Derrick had shown promising improvements, he still had a great deal to work on with his academic progress.

All Mr. Dinsmoor could say was that his son did not have a learning problem, and he was not going to stand by and see his son's name ruined and have him teased at school because he was in the dummy class! I knew Derrick didn't have that impression of my class and neither did his mother, so I immediately knew this opinion was only Mr. Dinsmoor's. He continued by stating that all his son needed to do was to work harder, and then he would do better.

The real shock was when he said it was obvious that his son was just lazy! (If Mr. Dinsmoor knew his son at all, lazy would never be a word to describe Derrick.) He then said he would continue to "ride" Derrick and make his punishments more severe. "That will correct the problem!" he declared. He sat there looking like Derrick's problem could be solved very simply. Just demand it to go away!

Now I understood why Mrs. Dinsmoor hadn't come to the meeting. She supported Derrick's placement in my class and probably anticipated her husband's scorching behavior and didn't want to be embarrassed when he made a scene. After I understood what Mr. Dinsmoor's true reason was for being at this conference, I thought in some ways he was possibly worse than fathers who were totally absent from the parenting situation. It was obvious that his ego was more important to him than getting assistance for his struggling son. This man didn't want to be embarrassed by Derrick's academic struggles. He really showed his ignorance of Derrick's situation and my class as a whole when he described it as a dummy class. Mr. Dinsmoor clearly didn't know how smart and capable his son was and that there were just some glitches in Derrick's learning style that were holding him back from progressing academically. Laziness was not the culprit and demanding better performance was not the solution!

Mr. Dinsmoor held a high position at IBM. It seemed to me that his son's struggles would not have fit the persona that he likely wanted to portray to his associates. His son in a special education class wouldn't make him look good. His fourth grade son was struggling with math, working on a first grade level, and yet was on grade level with his reading, and he wanted to pull Derrick from receiving help. None of what Mr. Dinsmoor was demanding made any sense. Derrick wanted to learn (thanks to Mrs. Dinsmoor) and worked very hard for both his regular classroom teacher and me. Because of his desire to learn and do well, along with the extra assistance, he had made wonderful progress, but there was a great deal more to do.

Mr. Dinsmoor continued his rant, admitting that from first grade on, Derrick's teachers reported that Derrick was slow in math and requested testing. He wouldn't hear of it. He knew his son was fine. "A Dinsmoor works out his own problems," he insisted vehemently. He said Derrick would just need to be disciplined more. The longer I listened, the more I was confused. How could such an educated man hold such an attitude? All I knew was that his pride was so blinding that he could not see how he was hurting his son.

When I thought Mr. Dinsmoor was finished with his tirade, I explained again what we had accomplished in my class and how much better Derrick was performing and feeling. I also added that he was accomplishing so much more in his regular classroom in just a few months. While I was still talking, Mr. Dinsmoor rudely interrupted me admitting that he knew all along it wouldn't work putting Derrick in a retarded class! It was as if the man hadn't heard a single thing I had said.

He continued by divulging that at the end of the previous school year, Derrick's difficult third grade, he had only agreed to have Derrick tested and to be enrolled in my class after his wife had pleaded with him. He claimed that Derrick was still having troubles (having only been in my program for three, yes three, months), and it was obvious to him that his son was wasting his time in my class. He demanded again that Derrick be removed immediately.

Still trying to be rational, I tried again to explain how far behind Derrick was and that with time and support, Derrick could do very well and be able to function much better in a regular classroom. Every time I spoke, Mr. Dinsmoor's eyes glazed over. Nothing I said seemed to sink in with him. When I finished speaking, he asked how in the world I could know what was best for his son since I was "young enough to still be in diapers!"

Granted I was young and had little in-class experience, but I knew, with all my heart, that Derrick needed help and that I would do whatever it took to help him. I agreed with Mr. Dinsmoor that I was young but added that I was confident that I could help Derrick. With that, Mr. Dinsmoor blew up at me. He bellowed that I had no idea what Derrick needed, and he angrily questioned, "How do I know you are qualified to have this conference, let alone work with my son?"

Now it was time to set this man straight! I never lost my temper but for just a moment I stared right at him giving myself time to think and get my composure. I agreed that he had every right to know my qualifications and took out a piece of paper. I explained my high grade point average in my major of special education. I wrote down the names of my professors and my student teaching supervisor. I told him that they all would be more than happy to talk with him about my abilities and qualifications to work with children. On that same sheet of paper, I wrote my social security number, the specific offices he should contact, and the main number to the university. Passing the paper to him, I requested that he call and have my records and qualifications as a teacher verified. Then, I turned the table on him.

I demanded to see his qualifications as a father. I added that based on the discussion we were having, he seemed ill-equipped for the job. He was making life unnecessarily difficult for his son due to his blinding pride. His pride wouldn't allow him to admit his son had a learning problem and that was going to keep his son from getting the help he needed. What he was doing to Derrick was deplorable and inexcusable. I added another jab by saying that he had been given ten years to help his son but unfortunately Derrick needed more help. It was now my turn to help Derrick!

I stopped talking but continued staring at him. Mr. Dinsmoor sat quietly, his eyes pulled away from mine to look down at the table. Trying to fill the awkward silence with more of an upbeat voice, I explained that Derrick would be so lucky if his mom *and* dad, along with the school, banded together to help him through this challenging time. The pressure resting on his young shoulders would be lifted because the unrealistic expectations wouldn't be weighing so heavily on him. Now that we could all work together (I figured I might as well assume that I had gotten through to him), we could expect a very happy and confident boy to arise. I admitted that no one could guarantee the level of progress Derrick would make, but I knew Mr. Dinsmoor would see many improvements with Derrick's work at school with him by his son's side. I also added that he might start having a better relationship with his son. In order to help Derrick though, the school and I needed time and his support. He lifted his eyes and looked at me with much softer eyes. After a few moments just looking at me, he agreed to give me the time and support because, despite what it seemed with his behavior, he truly wanted the best for his son.

Acknowledging his desire to help Derrick but still quite angry inside, I said that because of our discussion during this meeting, I would only continue working with Derrick if Mr. Dinsmoor would attend all the conferences, come to school for lunch at least once a month, and go on a few of the field trips with Derrick's regular classroom. I explained I wasn't trying to make life hard for him, but it was essential for him to learn how to help his son, and the best way for that to happen was to have him at the school participating in activities which involved Derrick.

Mr. Dinsmoor acknowledged that it would be difficult for him to get away from work, but he would manage somehow. With that, he asked when the next field trip was. After I wrote down the date for the field trip and handed Mr. Dinsmoor the paper, I knew it was time for this one hour and forty-five-minute conference to end. Extending my hand to shake Mr. Dinsmoor's hand, I thanked him for talking with me, and I truthfully stated how thrilled I was that we were now going to pull together to help Derrick. As we shook hands, Mr. Dinsmoor thanked me for my time and patience. Then he humbly added, "Now I understand why Derrick likes you so much!"

Anthony

DURING MY FINAL year teaching at this school, I had a few firsts: We had the trailer all to ourselves since the speech teacher was now based at another school, and I received my first handicapped child.

Anthony was a special child, and it wasn't because of his handicap. I remember distinctly how I felt the day I was told I would be receiving a fifth grader who was physically handicapped. Panic is a good descriptive word for those feelings. Believing I was not prepared to work with a handicapped child, I started searching for whatever legitimate reasons I could argue why I shouldn't have this child placed in my room. I never wanted to admit that I was afraid of him, or rather his handicap, so despite the fact that I didn't even know what Anthony's handicap was, I knew I didn't want "it" in my room.

I argued, thankfully, just for my ears to hear, that I had struggled for four and a half long years to develop my program to a point where it ran efficiently and effectively. And now this! It just wasn't fair to the other students or to me to turn everything upside down for just one student.

Oh my, what did all that sound like? Fortunately, I never uttered a word about my naive and unsubstantiated concerns and fears to anyone and welcomed Anthony into my program with an open mind and open heart. I quickly learned that with Anthony, handicap and all, there was nothing to fear and without a doubt, much to gain.

Before I met Anthony, I had received all of his school files. They were mainly filled with his medical background and very limited information concerning his educational needs. Most of the forms explained his medical struggles and were filled with numerous indecipherable medical terms. The gist of what I could understand was that Anthony had a growth problem. He was quite short yet his head was the size for a large man. His hands were the correct size for his head but his fingers were stubby and gnarled as if stricken with arthritis. His legs were terribly bowed and his feet were turned dramatically inward so he walked with a heavy and awkward gait.

What wasn't in his files was that Anthony was a bright, extremely witty, and happy young boy who just wanted to be treated like everyone else. Every hour that Anthony spent in my class was filled with good conversation, a desire for learning, hard work, enthusiasm, and laughter. He got along with everyone and seemed to love life. He also worked hard to please people so when he needed reprimanding, which was very seldom, it took all my strength not to give in because he truly hated to disappoint me or get scolded.

The students in my class became very protective of Anthony. None of them tolerated anyone in the school ridiculing him. Any teasing directed toward Anthony ended with a skirmish of varied size depending on who jumped in to protect Anthony. These situations subsided very quickly though because when the children in the rest of the school got to know Anthony, they just wanted to be his friend.

Since Anthony came to me as a fifth grader, I only had one very short year to work with him. During that time, he unknowingly taught me countless valuable lessons about life. One of the biggest lessons I needed to learn was never to assume someone knew something despite how simple it seemed to me.

From my work with kindergarteners, I knew that they loved and craved hugs. Since I believed my first and second graders probably still wanted hugs but might think they were too big now to get them, I would offer them hugs too, which they happily accepted. Then seeing that many of my other older students seemed to want hugs, I began offering hugs to anyone who wanted them.

I never made it mandatory and when I offered, most students readily accepted. The young students were always hungry for that physical attention so even if I forgot to give them a hug, these precious children never hesitated to come and *get a hug*. The older students may have been a little standoffish at first, but they grew to be quite comfortable with and look forward to our side hugs. On many occasions at the end of class, the students would even line up in front of me waiting their turn to give and get a hug before they returned to their regular classrooms.

It may have taken time for some students to feel at ease with hugs but everyone, even Anthony, came around to feel comfortable with hugs. Anthony was my hardest case to crack, though I would never have guessed why.

Time and time again, I would offer Anthony a hug and he would run screaming out of the classroom with giggles and defensive comments to keep me away. I honored his refusals with gentle words of understanding. Anthony's refusals went on and on, day after day. I never stopped offering him hugs, and he never stopped resisting them. That is until one day.

The final bell had rung and all the students had left except for Anthony. He was walking around the room muttering and (in my opinion) wasting time. Since I had so much schoolwork to correct from the day, I let him aimlessly wander around the room while I sat on a small chair as I worked at a low kidney-shaped table. I was totally engrossed in deciphering a student's handwriting when all of a sudden I felt a heavy weight land on my back. Along with the sudden impact,

I heard Anthony laughing. When I got my senses about me, I realized Anthony was leaning against my back, with all of his weight. It seemed obvious to me that Anthony had lost his footing and fallen. I rationalized that while he was trying to get his balance, he was laughing to cover up his embarrassment. For fear I would cause him to fall, I didn't move and calmly started talking to him in a moderate and reassuring tone. I tried to comfort him by saying that he would be all right, and I would help him stand back up whenever he was ready. As if he hadn't heard a single caring word I'd said, Anthony started talking about his day and asking me questions about specific assignments from class. Now this was very odd. What was going on?

Through numerous past experiences, I learned that there was always a reason for every peculiar act a child made. That was the easy part to grasp. The hard part to the mystery was to find out why he or she was acting a particular way and then offer a solution, if one was even necessary. As for the situation with Anthony, all I knew was that it was now obvious Anthony had not fallen. So why had this child decided to rest on my back? While we talked, I struggled to figure out Anthony's odd behavior. Finally, though it seemed quite far-fetched, I believed I had the answer to this bizarre situation but only because I couldn't think of any other reason.

I interrupted Anthony's monologue about his day and told him that he had hurt my feelings! I explained that he was not being fair to me, and I didn't like it. With his startled reaction, I prayed my theory was right. He immediately pleaded that he didn't mean to hurt my feelings and asked what he had done wrong. Still hoping I was right, I gingerly told him it was not fair that he got to give me a hug and I was not able to give him a hug. I explained the magic behind a real hug was that both people got to enjoy giving and getting the hug at the same time. Then I asked if he would allow me to give him a hug. His brief silence was broken with an ecstatic and determined, "Okay!"

I slowly sat straight up as Anthony pushed against my back to get to a standing position. Sitting in my chair, I pivoted around and was at eye level with Anthony. I asked if I could give him a hug at the same time he gave me a hug. Without a word, as if an emotional pressure valve burst inside him, Anthony flung his arms around me! He hit my head with his head, knocked off my glasses, and slapped my back. I ignored the pain in my head and didn't worry about my glasses; I just held onto Anthony as long as he held me, which was just a few seconds. As awkward (and painful) as this hug was, it was one of the most memorable hugs I ever received. After our hug, Anthony sat at the table with me for a short while, and we finished his conversation about his day and had a few laughs. When he left the room to catch his bus, I thanked him for my hug. He quickly smiled and then went running out of the room, but this time with just giggles. Progress!

Over the rest of the year, our hugs were more frequent, and Anthony became much more adept at giving them. He even got to the point where he was confident enough to come get a hug if I had forgotten to give him one. Now that was real success.

Who would have ever thought hugs needed to be taught? Thanks to Anthony, I learned that nothing could be taken for granted, even the simplest of acts like a hug!

Richard's Solution

EVERYONE CALLED HIM Buddy, but I just couldn't bring myself to use that name for a first grader. Mainly though, it just didn't fit him. I called him by his birth-given name, Richard. He never said anything to me about using this name, so I assumed it was all right with him. Evidently, it was more than all right.

After the issue concerning retention had been resolved and Richard was in the second grade, I had a parent/teacher conference with Richard's mom, Mrs. Mullen. During that conference, she confided a humorous story involving Richard's name. She explained that one afternoon the two of them were at home busy doing chores around the house. She wanted to get his attention, so she called him by his real name, Richard, the name she had given him. He surprised her with his response. He politely but emphatically told her that Richard was his special name and only Miss Chandler was allowed to use that name!

Thankfully, Mrs. Mullen was a great sport and graciously and lovingly obeyed his request. I also appreciated the fact that she held no animosity toward me with his request, and she actually thought it was rather cute! Later on, when Richard was in the third grade, he chose to allow Mrs. Martin to call him Richard also, making us the honored two who got to use that special name.

I had the privilege of working with Richard for five and a half years. Though I worked with a handful of other students that long and enjoyed my relationships with all of them, Richard was the only student who had me wrapped around his finger, but not in a spoiled way. For example, with his mother's blessing and classroom teacher's approval, if he wanted to stay in class an extra hour or two, I would always let him. He was able to accomplish and complete so much more in my room so when he was on a roll with some project or classwork, I hated to make him stop and would give in to his pleas to stay. His deep dimples, vibrant deep dark brown eyes, and his captivating smile melted my heart every time because they were all attached to his charming personality.

His teachers never minded me keeping Richard in my room because they were overloaded with students in their classes and to make special work for one student was more than they wanted to do. Richard always worked diligently in my room and though his progress was very slow, it was at least positive and steady. As long as his mom knew about *and* supported the extra time he spent with me, I didn't have a problem at all bending the rules.

After more than four years together, Richard and I knew each other's personalities pretty well. In so many ways, he felt like my own son, especially since we shared a few of the same personality traits. One trait we shared was that we were both extremely stubborn! Thankfully, in this situation, Richard was more persistent than I was.

One sunny fall day, when the school's schedule was jumbled yet again because of a school assembly, I found myself with more students in my room than I should have. Fifteen students and two adults may not sound overwhelming but finding room for seventeen people and all our stuff in such tiny quarters was quite challenging. Fortunately, we had seats for everyone, and all the students did their part to make our tight quarters work.

I know Anthony wouldn't have wanted his seizure to come on such a crowded day but then if he had a choice, I know he wouldn't have chosen to have a seizure at all. Everyone was busy working in small groups or on independent work when Anthony let out a startling scream. It was a frightening and frightened scream. Everyone turned to see what was wrong, only to witness Anthony in the beginning throes of a seizure-like attack.

As I had mentioned earlier, when Anthony came to our school, his student file was filled with many medical terms and reports. Not understanding some of what I read in Anthony's file, I had followed up with his pediatrician. He and I discussed many of Anthony's issues and challenges but one particular condition concerned me. I learned that he might have seizure-like attacks. The doctor calmed my nerves explaining that Anthony would *more than likely* never have these attacks *but* if the situation occurred, I was to simply calm him down and help him relax. The doctor suggested that I talk with Anthony in a quiet, controlled voice and get him in a comfortable position so the attack could pass. He assured me that nothing about the attack would be life threatening but his muscles would stiffen and cramp up, restricting Anthony's movements. The best way to help Anthony, the doctor repeated, was to keep him calm and comfortable until the attack passed.

The solution sounded simple and since the doctor wasn't concerned, neither was I. Unfortunately, believing the attack would never happen, I dismissed its seriousness. Sadly, I also had a false sense of security that if it did happen, it would be easy to handle. In reality, with fifteen students in a crowded trailer and me not having a clue what to do or the right words to say, Anthony's seizure was far from simple.

At first, all of my students were frightened by what they were witnessing and needed to be calmed down. Thankfully, Richard jumped into action to deal with his classmates, while I ran over to Anthony. As soon as I looked at him, his eyes locked onto mine. Though he couldn't speak at that moment, his eyes cried out, "Make it stop! Make it stop!" I quickly sat down next to him and pulled his shaking body on to my lap. I talked in a low soft voice while I rubbed his elbows and knees. I was doing everything I was told to do, but it wasn't working!

While Anthony was softly crying and moaning, I think more in fear than in pain, I whispered for him to lie on the floor where he could get comfortable and relax. Anthony immediately rejected my suggestion, mustering up whatever energy he could waste on me to beg, "No! No!"

I was too busy trying to do what *I* thought should be done instead of listening to what Anthony was saying and needing. All I knew was that I wanted to get him on the floor, but Anthony's screams got louder and louder with my continued suggestions. For the next minute or so, which seemed like an eternity, I tried to persuade him to stretch out on the floor, still only thinking of what I thought should happen. I even tried to bribe him by promising that he could lie down on the small mattress I kept in the back closet. (I know it sounds odd to have a mattress in a classroom closet but many times, when my students were sick, they either resisted going home or they couldn't go home. So for the just-kind-of-sick students, I would let them do their work while resting on the mattress.) In this particular situation though, nothing, even the offer of the highly coveted mattress, changed Anthony's determination to stay in his seat. His words were barely audible but the gist of what he was mumbling was that he wanted to sit up with everyone else. I was too busy making my solution work and too stubborn to listen to what Anthony was actually saying. Sadly, the whole time I was struggling with Anthony, I was only making matters worse.

Luckily for Anthony and me, Richard did listen and was there to help. He understood what Anthony needed, and he believed he had the real solution. Richard whispered in my ear, "Miss Chandler, I can help!" I thanked him but briskly brushed him off by saying, "No thank you, Richard. I have things under control." What a lie! It was obvious that I didn't have anything under control, but I said it anyway. Richard offered three more times, and I kept turning him down.

Only because I was so desperate and he was so determined did I finally, yet begrudgingly, accept his help.

I wrapped my arms around Anthony as he continued to shake, and together we watched Richard, a boy our school system labeled mildly educable mentally retarded, solve this problem so simply and effortlessly. Richard found the correct solution because he listened to what Anthony had been saying. At this point, all I needed to do was watch while the room got a facelift.

Richard politely directed all the students to push their desks quickly and quietly to the walls of the trailer, opening a large area in the room. He helped the students place their books, papers and pencils, side by side, neatly on the floor. Then he instructed them all to lie down on the floor and get back to work! There were a few comical facial expressions as these children looked to me for clarification, but I just supported Richard by telling them to do what he instructed them to do. Richard proceeded to get everyone settled on the floor. I was amazed by his ingenuity and my stupidity.

Carrying the mattress, Richard ran over to where Anthony and I were. He placed the mattress on the floor right in front of Anthony. Richard announced to the other students that everyone would get a chance to lie on the mattress, but Anthony was first! With that, he helped me lay the very willing Anthony on the mattress. In between his cries and moans, we actually heard him snicker a few times! When Anthony was properly positioned on the floor, Richard took his place right next to his friend.

Looking around my room, I marveled at how quickly it had been transformed. Thankfully, since Anthony was more comfortable, he had stopped crying and was now able to relax. Breathing a sigh of relief, I grabbed a tissue to dry my face. Then I did the only thing left to do and that was, dress and all, take my place on the floor.

Thanks to Richard hearing and understanding that Anthony didn't want to be different from his classmates any more than he already was, Richard solved this problem by putting us all on the floor so Anthony wouldn't be different. The amazing thing about this whole situation was that we accomplished the same classwork while working on the floor that we would have sitting in our seats.

I am happy to say that Anthony never had another attack while he was at our school. I was so grateful that Richard was there when Anthony did have his attack since he proved to be the more mature one and actually listened to what Anthony was saying. Keep in mind Richard was only eleven! Richard's solution not only helped Anthony through his frightening attack but it also allowed Anthony to hold on to his dignity. In addition to demonstrating ingenuity and determination, Richard also displayed valuable aspects of true friendship—a caring and listening heart coupled with thoughtful action!

For the Love of Running

"OKAY!" I ANNOUNCED, and Craig ran outside of the classroom to his starting point on the playground. With my stopwatch in hand, I yelled through the open window, "On your mark, get set, GO!" and off Craig sprinted along his designated route, which was the basic shape of a baseball diamond. As I watched him run, I marveled at his stride, form, and especially his enthusiasm for running.

Although my classroom was upgraded from a condemned, old trailer to just an old trailer, it was still placed right by the playground which meant the windows on one side of the trailer still had a view of the playground. Normally, the view was a distraction but for this situation, it was a real benefit. As Craig ran his course, I kept his classmates informed of his split times while they watched him through the windows. When he came around to the last leg of the course, the other children started to cheer louder and louder for him. He was running at a good pace but the last leg was up hill. We all saw that he was getting tired, but his smile was still strong. Craig enthusiastically ran over the finish line and all the children roared with excitement and applauded, especially when he bounded into the classroom. He quickly asked what his time was and looked over to see what I had posted on his chart. Craig and everyone else saw he had missed his best time by five seconds. Acknowledging the slower time, all Craig said was that after the next math page, he would get another chance to beat his time.

Craig's passion was running. Fifth grade was very challenging and though he tolerated academics, they were very difficult for him. When Craig reached his limit with frustration, he would just shut down, so I used his love of running to motivate him not only to do his work, but to do it well. When he did one page of math or two pages of language arts or read four pages in his reading book, answering comprehension questions and achieving at least eighty-five percent accuracy in any of those assignments, he got to run.

When Craig earned the privilege to run, I would time how long it took him to run the whole course, then I would jot the splits and final time on a sheet of paper for him to see. When I first started, I literally just counted in my head as he ran and told him the estimated time. Never did I imagine where this idea would take us. I quickly learned he genuinely wanted to know his actual times so I bought a stopwatch that allowed me to record his times more precisely. The other students got so interested in Craig's accomplishments that he thoughtfully requested that I post his times on the board so everyone could see them. That way, he wouldn't have to constantly repeat his times to every classmate who inquired. Oh, the price of fame! Instead of writing them on the board, I decided to record his times on a large wall poster so we could track his progress.

This whole running idea morphed out of pure desperation as I tried to get Craig to do his classwork. Based on what had worked successfully in the past with other students, I learned what Craig enjoyed spending his time doing and then figured out how to use that interest to encourage him to do what I wanted. Simple? Not on your life. This time it may have worked out better and faster, but it was only because I had learned through many other children and on many other occasions as I tried to accomplish my objectives: get the child to learn what he or she was supposed to learn as well as help the child enjoy the process of learning.

When I first started the running program, it was warm outside and quite a novelty to all my students. Others wanted to be included in the running program, and I let them, but it didn't take long for most of the children to tire of it. For some, it only took one run but for others, it took a couple days. Anthony was the one who held out the longest. When he first asked to participate, I immediately wanted to protect him and say no, but in the end, I let him partake in the fun. Having learned to listen to what Anthony was saying, I respected his request. That being said, I never required or discouraged anyone to run. They decided on their own. Craig was the only one willing to suffer the elements to continue his quest for a faster time.

I wish I knew when it happened, but over time, as Craig gradually began achieving more success with his assignments, he stopped asking to run as often and eventually stopped asking to run at all during class. He still had an incredible love for running, but he opted to improve his times during recess. Evidently, he had found a new challenge and sense of enjoyment as he experienced a new love—a love of learning.

Craig's Christmas Gift

CRAIG ALWAYS LIT up our classroom whenever he entered it. Not because he was gregarious or the class clown because he was neither. Instead, he was quiet, gentle, and extremely kind. It was the air or spirit he brought in with him that was so uplifting. Though Craig had serious academic challenges, he seemed to love being in my room. I might have difficulty getting some students to my room but with Craig, that was never a problem. He was always at my door on time or early. The problem I had with him was when it was time for him to leave.

When the time was approaching for him to return to his regular classroom, he would conjure up an excuse like needing more time to complete his work or he would act like he didn't understand something and ask for more help. One of his most creative ploys was to beg to stay longer since it was important for him to help a classmate (usually the closest person to him that he could grab and act like he was helping) with his or her work. When he was really desperate for an excuse to stay, he would even claim that he needed to clean his desk! I knew that was a stretch for Craig because he and I had the same neat-o-meter that meant everything went into a pile, and we were happy. For a while, I fell for the sweet yet devious ploys since I truly enjoyed having him in my room, but I knew a line had to be drawn. For most of the days, I drew that line, and I would have to gently threaten him to get him to leave. On my weak days though, I would allow him to stay much longer than he was supposed to and thankfully, his regular classroom teacher never minded because she knew he would be doing work on his ability level and not be frustrated as he always was in her room.

I had the privilege to work with Craig for almost two years, which meant we shared two Christmases together. I love Christmas and other holidays but as a teacher, the holidays were never popular with me because they interrupted the flow of my program. Consistency was crucial with all of my students. Holidays caused chaos and disruptions for my students and me due to our daily schedules being jumbled up by assemblies and added activities.

Christmas, as other holidays, came with the regular interruptions, but it had the extra distraction of gift giving. It never mattered how many times I told my students they were not to give me a present on any occasion, including Christmas, invariably, a few students would still bring in gifts. I quickly made a policy that I would never open a gift in front of the students since it could put pressure on the other children who didn't bring in a gift. During the Christmas season, I was lucky since I could simply explain that I was going to save my presents and open them on Christmas day. Thankfully, all of my students, minus one, accepted this rationale.

Over the first Christmas Craig and I shared, a few students did give me some gifts and though I was very discrete receiving them, I could tell Craig was deeply bothered that he didn't have anything to give me. I would tell him, along with all of my students that they were my gift every day they walked into my room. I truly meant it. All the other students accepted my declaration with giddy smiles but not Craig. He might give me a little grin, but I could tell the situation truly bothered him as he recoiled in what seemed to be a state of embarrassment. Just as he demonstrated with his academic determination, he must have decided that he was not going to endure this embarrassment again, and he made sure of it the following Christmas.

On the last day of school before the Christmas holiday, we always had a party after lunch with students who could attend. The food and decorations were abundant and the moods were always cheerful and enthusiastic as we played games (educational ones of course!). Few, if any, of my students would come to my room before lunch because they were busy in their regular classes cleaning their rooms and desks, preparing for the long Christmas break.

Early that morning, when no one was in my room, Craig came in to see me. In his hands, he held a package that was roughly wrapped in used Christmas paper. He proudly handed it to me, showing off his precious Cheshire smile. He was incredibly eager for me to see what was inside his package, so he politely pleaded, as he jumped up and down, for me to open it right away. Thinking the situation over and realizing that no one else was in the room, I agreed.

In anticipation, Craig's facial expressions were comical. Enjoying his excitement, I took my time unwrapping his gift, which proved to be difficult since there was no tape used. Having drawn out the unwrapping process as much as possible, I finally revealed his gift. In my hand, I held a piece of wood about one and a half inches square by three and a half inches long. I wasn't sure what the gift was but in its original use the block of wood had been stained a dark brown. The wood had recently been roughly cut on one end. On the other end, was a hole about one third of an inch wide and about two inches deep with small indentations around the hole. Craig couldn't contain his excitement anymore and yelled out, "How do you like it? How do you like it?"

I was enjoying Craig's enthusiasm more than the present because I really didn't know what it was supposed to be. I had at least realized what it had been, but I was struggling to grasp what he wanted it to be now. There was no way I was going to hurt his feelings so I knew I had to decipher this mystery. In order to steal some extra time to think, I teased him in a whimsical way as I silently asked myself what in the world the wood was supposed to be. Happily, the answer came to me. I walked to my desk and picked up a pen. I set the block on my desk with the rough end down and put the pen in the exposed hole. Craig jumped up and down, happily probing how I liked his gift. When he calmed down, after hearing how touched and thrilled I was with his gift, he unveiled the whole story of how my gift came to be.

Craig had found an old chair in a dump near his neighborhood and took it home. His dad let him use the handsaw to cut off the end of one leg. Then Craig pried out the metal tack that the chair rested on. That accounted for the exposed hole (where my pen went) and indentations around it. Then he told me how he got the wrapping paper out of the Christmas ornament box at his house. Evidently, his mother used old Christmas paper to cushion their ornaments when they were being stored. Craig described how he got the paper and spread it out as best he could and then wrapped up his penholder. He admitted that he couldn't find any tape so he just rolled it up as tightly as he could.

I was extremely touched hearing the trials Craig went through in order to give me a gift. When he finished his story, he tentatively inquired again what my thoughts were toward his gift. Giving him a huge hug, I told him quite honestly it was one of the most wonderful gifts anyone had ever given me. I elaborated by saying that he had actually given me two presents because the story of how he made the penholder was also a special gift!

From that day on, Craig's penholder was proudly displayed at my workstation in the middle of our classroom. Though no one knew where it came from or how I got it, everyone knew it was special to me. What was so much fun about Craig's gift was that if he came into my room and saw the holder empty, he immediately went on a hunt to find a pen to place in the hole. One day I asked him why it was so important that a pen had to be kept in his holder. In an effort to keep our gift giving event a secret, Craig whispered in my ear that he needed to make sure everyone knew what the holder was for because they might not be as smart as I was!

I know Christmas doesn't come in a package, but for this particular Christmas, that package held what Christmas represents. It wasn't what was in the package; it was the love that was represented by the gift: the genuine thought, effort, and emotions that went into the physical gift made it a true Christmas gift. Sadly, I am not sure what happened to my penholder but magically, just like Christmas, the love and admiration from that gift, still warm my heart. Now that is a true Christmas gift!

Rosella

ROSELLA'S STAY AT our school was only temporary because she was waiting for an opening in a self-contained classroom for the severely emotionally handicapped, which our school didn't provide. While she was waiting for an opening, administrators in the Central Office placed her at our school in a regular third grade classroom with twenty-six students, one teacher, and a part-time aide. Of course, a regular classroom would be a logical place to put her since she had been diagnosed as severely emotionally handicapped! There was absolutely no logical rationale for this placement. Did they think Rosella would just act as if she had no problems until she was placed in the proper classroom? For a few days after arriving at our school, Rosella actually did *act* like she didn't have any problems. That was until one day when she let everyone in the school and parts of the neighborhood know she was desperately in need of help.

It was late in the morning and the unrelenting sun was beaming down on our trailer when I got my first glance at Rosella. As usual, our air conditioner was not working, so our windows and doors were all wide open. I only had six students in the room at that particular time, and we were enjoying a fun group project when we started hearing this horribly painful wail come from the main building. The crying kept on with great intensity, and it continued for so long that I gave up thinking a teacher in the building would help the poor child. I left my class with Mrs. Martin in charge and followed the mournful sobbing. It wasn't hard to locate. Two rooms into the building, I found the noise coming from Mrs. Galloway's room. As I got closer, I could hear other sounds of commotion along with the cries of despair. As I looked through the doorway, there before me was pure chaos. Mrs. Galloway and Mr. Briggs seemed to be in a confused and frustrated state with the backdrop of students clamoring around and staring at something on the floor. There in the corner of the room was a poor child curled up as tightly as she could physically be. She looked like she was trying to hide from someone or something but not necessarily from anyone in the classroom. Tears were streaming down her face. Mucus was dripping from her nose and she sat in a puddle of urine. She wailed with such emotional pain that it was somewhat eerie. It didn't matter how much I wanted to help her, I knew I would only make matters worse if I tried to get involved at this point. As I stood there, other teachers started coming to the door. Trying to do what I could to help, I simply told these teachers that everything was being handled and shut the door, allowing for some privacy so Mrs. Galloway and Mr. Briggs could help the little girl. As I walked back to my class, I listened to her cry. It seemed like she was crying because of something deeper than whatever happened at school. Later, I learned that this precious child experienced more pain and suffering in her eight short years than the average person experiences in a long lifetime.

When school had been dismissed, I went to the office to inquire about the child, her background and to ask why I hadn't been notified about her. Mr. Briggs, whom I had great admiration for, said the little girl's name was Rosella. He was as surprised as I was with her placement and had called Cen-

tral Office to get some answers. Unfortunately, Mr. Briggs
didn't have much to go on since her files hadn't been received
at our school yet. With his inquiry to her old school, he was
told that since my room was at its maximum limit and the
people at Central Office knew it was only a temporary placement, they didn't think putting Rosella in a regular classroom
would be a problem. I will never understand why the administration chose to say my class was full at this particular time. If
she needed self-contained placement and there were no open-
ings and my class was full, putting her in a regular class only
meant that some group of overpaid out-of-touch administrators did not think through their solution. The placement was
not even remotely fair to Rosella, the other students, or the
teacher. Sadly, it wasn't until two more unnecessary situations
occurred, that the Central Office administrators magically
approved temporary placement for Rosella in my room, even
though I was still at "capacity" but now they said I had room!

Rosella's placement in my room was still not a good
option because she had to get used to leaving one room and
going to another. This can be quite disrupting to some students with certain problems. My class was definitely better
than nothing though because it kept her from feeling the
pressures of a large classroom all day. Mrs. Galloway and I
worked it out that in addition to her scheduled times to see
me, if Rosella needed to leave her regular classroom or Mrs.
Galloway needed her to leave, Rosella had a place to find some
peace and quiet.

Surprisingly, I never once had a problem with Rosella in
my classroom. She worked hard, helped others, demonstrated
wonderful manners, and was an extremely neat and organized
person. She seemed to love being in my room and, as Rosella
settled into our routine, Mrs. Galloway and I would allow
her to stay as long as she wanted or needed but making sure
she didn't take advantage of us either. Knowing she worked
better with small groups, on occasions, as with other students

I served, Mrs. Galloway and I conveniently forgot the time limit rule for my room and allowed her to stay all day.

From reading her confidential files and talking with Rosella, I learned about her very difficult life. At birth, she was an alcoholic and addict. She was beaten so badly one time that the right side of her face was slightly but permanently sunken in. She was used repeatedly in drug exchanges as an infant and care for her health and safety in these exchanges was never a concern. Her mother over-dosed when Rosella was still an infant, but her father, a self-proclaimed part-time minister, married a woman who had habits much like Rosella's birth mother. The father had no formal pastoral training, yet he took it upon himself to say God was talking through him and people should listen to what he had to say. Everything he did, according to him, was in the name of God. Proclaiming this status pulled the wool over many people's eyes, and he got away with a great deal, but I'm certain God didn't approve.

Once a psychologist innocently told the father that Rosella needed to cry and experience the pain she was keeping inside. The psychologist said that crying would help her heal by releasing all the pent-up emotions from the painful situations Rosella had been through. Months before we met Rosella, the father, hearing this information from the psychologist, got his part-time parish together and decided he was going to do some part-time ministering and demand his daughter to cry. This had to have been confusing for Rosella since prior to this, her father had forbidden her to cry saying it was a sign the devil was in her. He managed to convince his followers to gather around her creating a circle with Rosella in the middle. Then they proceeded to shove her back and forth between them screaming and yelling for her to cry. I guess this time to let the devil out! Who knows the reasoning the father used to get his worshippers to do this but according to the social worker, these screaming sessions happened several times but to no avail. Rosella never cried; she just withdrew even more. She didn't cry, that is, until the infamous day in Mrs. Galloway's classroom. At that time, she must have met all the fears, sorrows, and pains she had ever felt. No one knew what set Rosella off that day, but just maybe the psychologist was right and she needed to let it all out. She just needed to do it on her own terms.

Pretend With Rosella

I LEARNED VERY early in my teaching experience that I had just a few seconds to evaluate the attitude level of a student when he or she walked into my classroom. That instant evaluation would determine how I would teach and what I would teach that day. I prepared for each student every day, but I had to stay flexible. Daily, I hoped to at least teach the skill I had planned but sometimes even that would change because of circumstances out of my control. Drawing on what I learned from Dr. Coble and Miss Watkins, I learned to teach whatever and however I could whenever I could. Sometimes what I needed to teach and actually taught had nothing to do with academics and was possibly even more important!

One very special afternoon I was given the privilege to spend some one-on-one time with Rosella. After lunch, there was an assembly for most of the students. That meant my classes were, yet again, all jumbled, and I found myself with no students—until Rosella walked in. Her stride told me that no academic skill was going to be taught that day and that turned out to be right. She entered the classroom full of energy and conversation though saying nothing special, just general talk. After a while, she slowed down and finally complained about being sleepy. Through a variety of questions, I learned that Rosella's step-mother had kept her up all night until the wee hours of the morning because she wanted Rosella to keep her company! That meant that Rosella only had a few hours of sleep. Seeing how sleepy Rosella was, I asked her to sit on my lap and suggested that we just talk some more. Her buck-toothed smile always melted my heart and with my invitation, that smile was immediately inches away from my face when she jumped up on my lap.

I started gently rocking her as we began sharing many stories. Rosella brought up the subject of families. She shared several incidents she'd had with her two mothers and her dad. None were pleasant and some were heartbreaking. Though she was getting sleepier and sleepier, she kept talking. Out of nowhere, she found some energy and sat straight up. She looked right at me and confessed that she wished she had a *real* mom, a nice and loving mom. Not knowing what else to say, I admitted to her that I wished I had a daughter. With that, she quietly cradled herself back in my arms. After a few moments of silence, I whispered in her ear that maybe for that afternoon she and I could have our wishes. I told her that we could pretend, just for that time, I was her mom and she was my daughter. It would be our secret! She sat up again, held my hands tightly looking at me with that huge melt-your-heart smile and said she loved that idea and she would never tell! She cradled herself back in my arms, and I held her gently and began quietly humming a made-up tune. After a few min-utes, Rosella started talking about adventures we could have together, but she became sleepy and fell sound asleep after a few moments.

In no time, she was in a heavy, relaxed state, maybe because she felt safe and just let go. I have no idea how long we were like this since my wall clock was broken, and I wasn't wearing my watch, but I knew it was long enough for my tears to dry up on their own since my arms were holding Rosella, and I had no way of wiping my face without possibly disturbing her. It was some time after this I heard my other students coming toward the trailer. I never expected them to respond the way they did, but I guess it was their turn to view a situation and adapt their behavior accordingly. I was so proud of how they read the situation and reacted.

Richard and Colton came in first and wanted to know why the lights were off. As soon as they saw Rosella in my arms, they quickly dropped their voices and alerted the others coming in to be quiet. I never asked them to do anything special. Actually, I was trying to figure out how I was going to wake up Rosella, but I never had to because my wonderful students tiptoed in and since they all knew their routines in class they got right to work. When anyone needed help, there was a classmate nearby to give the needed assistance. If a question couldn't be answered with the help of others, that child came to me and asked his or her question as softly and quietly as possible. Once I answered too loudly, and Richard actually shushed me. I don't know for sure, but it seemed the children sensed that Rosella needed the attention and sleep, and they were ready and willing to help. I rarely treated my students alike since their needs were so different, and I always hoped they saw that though their treatments were different, it was always fair. This day showed me that they not only saw the differences, they understood and supported them.

My right arm had gone totally numb and was now in the burning stage, but I didn't dare move for fear of waking Rosella or disappointing the other students since they had worked so hard to allow her to sleep. The situation might have been sweet, but I have to admit I was relieved when the dismissal bell finally rang since my arm was in a great deal of pain. Instead of the loud clamoring at the sound of the bell, this time all the students tiptoed around putting their books and papers away. As they left the trailer, they took turns and gave me side hugs and softly whispered their good-byes.

When silence returned, I could hear Rosella's heavy breathing. Sadly, I knew I had to wake her up from her deep sleep because she couldn't miss her bus. Quietly, I called her name over and over until she slowly started to move around. When she finally opened her eyes, the grin on her face seemed to light up the room. Rosella was surprised to hear what time it was so she jumped off my lap and scurried around to get ready to leave. While she got herself organized, I gingerly started moving my arm to get the circulation back in it. Rosella was rushing out of the room when she realized she had forgotten to get her hug from me, so she hustled over and with great enthusiasm, gave me an energetic hug around my neck. She whipped around toward the door to leave but stopped and turned around again. With giddiness about her, Rosella thanked me for being her mother for the afternoon. She cocked her head and bared her adorable buck-toothed smile announcing that I was going to make a great real mom someday. I thanked her for being my daughter and emphasized she was already a great real daughter. She responded by flashing that wonderful smile with an added giggle and said she'd see me in the morning. Then she ran out the door as abruptly as she had entered a few hours earlier.

Rosella may not have been taught any academics that day but hopefully she learned and felt what real love was.

Rosella Was Late

IT WAS EIGHT-THIRTY A.M. and Rosella was nowhere to be found. Where was she? Even though Rosella had to get herself up, dress and feed herself, then catch the bus all on her own since her father and step-mother were out of the house long before she awoke, she never missed school and was never late. Rosella never missed school for many reasons. The main reason was that she knew her parents would never tolerate any excuse for missing school, and a beating was inevitable if she ever did. Consequently, Rosella would arrive in all states of health, dress, and with or without sleep or food. She always caught the bus. So where was she today? Rosella was one of my students I worried about constantly because of her home situation. Though her case was actively being reviewed by social services to remove her from the home, it didn't keep me from worrying at that moment. I knew there was a problem, but I didn't know what to do.

The first bell rang. Rosella always visited me before the first bell. Then the second and last bell rang. No Rosella. Something was definitely wrong. I tried using our intercom system to ask our secretary to call Rosella's house just in case she had overslept, but there was no answer from the office. Time crept

by as I worried and imagined all types of problems Rosella
could have encountered. Death was always a possibility. At
nine o'clock, I knew I had to call the social worker and ask
her to go by the house. She and I understood that calling the
parents was never a choice, since the call itself could create
a serious problem for Rosella. There was no reason to cause
alarm if there was a simple explanation for Rosella's absence.
Since no one was answering the intercom call in the office,
I told my students that I needed to go to the office to call
the social worker, which would leave them unsupervised. In
today's school rules, that would have been a real 'no-no,' but
my students all knew it was unusual for Rosella not to be in
class, and they realized she needed help. As I left the room,
my students reassured me that they would be able to take care
of things while I was gone, and I knew they would. I learned,
through this occasion and many others over the years, that
students live up to what is expected of them so it was no surprise that my students handled themselves quite well while I
was gone.

I never wore a coat when I walked between my trailer
and the school building, despite the icy cold winter weather,
because I didn't want to carry a coat around while I was in
the building. That morning, it was bitterly cold, so I walked
quickly. As I headed toward the ramp to the building, I heard
the rumble of an old Volkswagen coming into the faculty
parking lot. Wanting to avoid a possible conversation, I looked
away from the car and walked even faster.

As I was halfway up the ramp, I heard my name being called
from the direction of the parking lot and instinctively turned
around. I was totally surprised and relieved to see Rosella. She
was smiling through the window of the Volkswagen that had
just driven up and was enthusiastically waving at me. When the
car stopped, the door opened and out came a pair of old brown
tattered slip-on shoes, two sized too big for the feet in them—
and no socks! Rosella's knobby legs were bare. Her body was

clad in a short sleeve summer dress one or two sizes too small—
and no coat. Her big buck-toothed smile was such a contrast to
her poor attire and the severity of her situation.

I will never forget the overwhelming relief and joy I felt
seeing her beautiful smile, but I also will remember how the
tears cooling on my face reminded me how cold the morning was. Because of her shoes, Rosella clumsily ran up to me
and wrapped her arms around my hips squeezing as tightly as
she could and asked with excitement if I had missed her and
was I glad to see her. I returned her hug with just as much
enthusiasm and answered her questions with all affirmatives.
Through her excitement, she mumbled that the woman in
the car wanted to talk with me so I walked over to the car
with Rosella hanging on around my waist. The woman was
in her mid-thirties and was smiling through the car window.
She introduced herself and explained that she was driving to
work and saw this child, poorly dressed for the weather, walking in the freezing cold. She stopped to question the girl and
fortunately for Rosella, the woman was kind and harmless.
Plus, she even worked in the main office of the Department of
Education. She knew no child should be out walking around
at nine A.M. and planned on taking Rosella either to school or
back to Rosella's house. With those choices, Rosella strongly
requested to go to school. Saying thank you just didn't seem
enough to explain how grateful I was for this woman's kindness, but I still kept babbling, "Thank you!" over and over. The
woman seemed satisfied enough to see Rosella was safe and
welcomed so warmly, so she went on her way.

Walking to our classroom, I told Rosella that I wanted to
hear all about her adventure but she had to wait until we were
in the room. I knew Rosella was supposed to go to her regular
classroom, but I needed to spend some time with her. I knew
her regular classroom teacher wouldn't mind.

As soon as we got into the classroom, I used the intercom to call the secretary to let her know that Rosella was at

school and in my room. I also asked if she would let Rosella's classroom teacher know Rosella was at school. While I was talking with the secretary, Rosella skipped and hopped around the room with all types of facial expressions and enthusiasm. It was obvious that it wasn't because of her adventure but because she was *home* with the people who loved her.

When I got off the intercom, it was time to hear Rosella's story. With constant prodding throughout her entire story, it seemed that her morning started abruptly because she had overslept. The bus was long gone when Rosella woke up so she dressed as quickly as possible, running out of the house without food or proper clothing. In her mind, she knew she had to get to school no matter what. Though I am sure Rosella wanted to avoid a beating from her parents, she was also very concerned about the possibility of missing her friends and our school activities.

Rosella's story was quite simple yet potentially very dangerous. Her school bus was for special education children being brought in from other school districts. That meant the bus went in all different neighborhoods, some of them being quite a distance from the school. Because of where she lived, Rosella was always the first to be picked up and since she didn't know the direct route to get to school, she had started walking the way the bus went every morning! Hearing where Rosella had been picked up by this wonderful Good Samaritan, she had to have been walking about fifteen or twenty minutes in the freezing cold. No telling how many people drove by her turning a blind eye to her situation or who were just too busy to lend a hand to a lost and ill-clad child! Thanks to a kind and caring person who took time to help a child, Rosella was not cold for long and my Rosella was *home* and safe.

Rosella's Doll

I COULDN'T TAKE it any longer. I had to call and see how Rosella was doing. It had been a month since she had been placed in her self-contained classroom for severely emotionally handicapped children. Not only was I worried and concerned, I missed her.

Ironically, the summer before I met Rosella, I was in a teachers' workshop and her future self-contained classroom teacher was in the same workshop. I had been impressed with what I heard from this man as he actively participated in the workshop, never knowing I would be working with Mr. Jordan in the future. He truly seemed to care about his students, and it sounded as if he had a great deal of success with them. When I heard Rosella was placed in Mr. Jordan's class, I was relieved because I felt he genuinely would take the necessary time to work with Rosella's needs.

When I called the school where Mr. Jordan worked, I knew I would have to leave a message. It took him a day to return my call, which I understood since call-backs were always difficult for me too. When we eventually talked, Mr. Jordan was so grateful that I was interested in Rosella's progress, and he didn't mind at all catching me up with what she was doing and accomplishing. Interestingly, if he had returned my call the day before, I would never have learned what happened that particular day.

There had been an assembly organized by the physical education department for the third and fourth graders the morning he called me back. For one of the many activities during the assembly, students were asked to volunteer to tell a story of a time when they had to compete. They were supposed to include in their story what they had done, what it was like, and how they felt about the end result. Each child who volunteered was to go in front of approximately two hundred students and tell his or her story.

The physical education teacher had asked for volunteers the day before to allow the children time to think about what they would like to say. With some encouragement from Mr. Jordan, Rosella volunteered to tell a story. We both knew she could tell a great story, but he must have done a wonderful job encouraging her to speak in front of so many people. That was such a big step for her since she was very reserved in front of small groups of people, let alone a crowd!

When it was her turn to speak, Mr. Jordan said she didn't hesitate to walk right up in front of all of her classmates. Evidently, she hopped up on the provided stool and looked out on the audience with her famous ear-to-ear buck-toothed smile. Initially, she hemmed and hawed a bit but she finally got on track and started talking. She spoke as if she was talking to a group of her best friends instead of an auditorium full of students. Mr. Jordan described her as being very confident and said she seemed to love being in front of the crowd and was excited to tell her story.

Very briefly, her story was about Field Day when she was enrolled at my school. During Field Day, she had to compete with her classmates in a relay race. Mr. Jordan said she didn't talk long, but she did a great job, and I would have been very proud of her.

As a side bar to his story, he added what made her speech so sweet was that she insisted on taking her adorable bright red, fuzzy ball-doll up with her. The fuzzy ball, about ten inches in diameter, had a big smiley face on it made from felt material. Mr. Jordan said the ball-doll was exceptionally cute and cuddly looking and went on to explain that every day since she arrived at his school, this fuzzy doll came with her. Wherever she went, the ball-doll went. During the assembly, Mr. Jordan described her holding it in the crook of her arm with a very firm hold. As she talked, she rubbed the fuzzy ball. He believed the fuzzy ball gave her the confidence to do such a great job in front of all the other students. We talked quite a while before Mr. Jordan had to get back to his class. Before we said goodbye, I quickly thanked him for taking such good care of Rosella and added that I knew she was in good hands.

After I hung up, I reached for the tissues that I always kept in my pocket to dry my face and tried to get my composure back. Thankfully, we were on the phone and not in person so Mr. Jordan didn't see me crying at the end of our conversation. I wasn't sad. Actually, I was filled with joy and relief. My Rosella was happy and doing well—and she seemed to love the adorable, bright red, fuzzy ball smiley-faced doll that I had given her on her last day in my classroom. I had been given the ball-doll as a gift from my parents when I was thirteen because I loved smiley faces. Handing it to Rosella on her last day with me, I explained that I wanted her to have something of mine to remind her how much I loved her and how proud I was of her. Never in my wildest dreams could I have imagined that she needed the doll maybe as much as I needed to give it to her!

Spit Bucket

WHEN I FIRST started teaching, I had been warned how the hot southern springs were notorious for creating obnoxious tyrants out of the best students and short-tempered teachers out of the most patient, but I didn't think it could be that bad. How wrong I was! After experiencing my first disastrous spring with chaos, it was easy to understand why no one, student or teacher, could get excited over stale books when they had to sit in a sweltering small classroom with sweaty classmates and no air movement. It was obvious that we needed something exciting and different to do so we could all survive our second spring together, but I was fresh out of ideas. Thanks to a terrific coworker and friend, I was introduced to hatching eggs.

Hatching eggs sounded like a perfect solution for my fast approaching second spring dilemma. There was one minor obstacle: I didn't know anything about hatching eggs. Fortunately for me, there was endless information available at the school and public libraries, so I learned quickly how to get started, and I definitely felt well prepared for our spring event.

Since I had my students year after year, I only planned on doing this project for that particular spring. Little did I know we would be starting a yearly trend in our classroom. My students were so captivated by what they experienced with our first go-round, they insisted on hatching eggs over the next four springs!

Each February, following our first successful journey hatching eggs, my students would start imagining and talking about all the experiences they might have during the upcoming egg hatching spring project. They would also reminisce about the many and varied events that took place the year and years before. Then, what I really loved was witnessing the creativity that surfaced from my students when they started conjuring up their own activities involving the hatching process and the birds.

I believe none of us got tired of this project because we were always totally involved with hatching the eggs. We didn't have a learning center in a corner of the classroom that had an incubator with eggs in it and magically one day birds appeared and then they were looked at once in a while. In our class, we centered around the eggs and birds. From the youngest student to the oldest, everyone took part. We studied, wrote, and talked about eggs, birds, equipment, and responsibilities. Stories and poems were written and illustrated, storybooks and science books were read, and questions and answers were discussed.

Even though the librarian was never thrilled about my students being in the library, we went to it often for this and many other projects. I may not have personally liked the librarian, but I had to admit she did an excellent job with the library. She made sure her library was well stocked with awesome books, and my class and I definitely benefited from all of her work.

As a resource teacher, I learned that the books in the library were always more helpful than any of my textbooks so it was my favorite place to get great material for my students. The library was also the place where our incubator was stored. What a sight that incubator was! It was a large, alien looking, obsolete contraption made out of aluminum with a terribly scratched plastic section on the top posing as a window. We did have two newer incubators but they went to teachers who had seniority over me. The incubator I was to use looked like it should have been thrown out but thankfully, no one had. Though there were many idiosyncrasies about this contraption, I didn't complain because it worked.

The learning curve for what we were to do with the incubator and eggs was quite steep our first year. A friend who raised chickens gave us ten eggs that had been candled verifying that they were fertile eggs. I placed the incubator right in the middle of our room, and it was ready to house our eggs. We had marked opposite sides of each egg with an *x* and an *o* so we could keep track of the egg position as we turned them. After the students had endured many long monologues from me about how accurately and gently the eggs and incubator were to be handled, everyone got to help turn the eggs.

I endlessly repeated to all my students, that it was their responsibility to keep track of the egg-turning schedule. At first, I thought my sage words (more like obnoxious words) had made an impact on them but I came to realize that my students *saw the need*, and they filled it. A group of my older students even decided to create their own, more accurate schedule for turning the eggs and posted it on the chalkboard. They even drew up a time schedule to check the temperatures and water level of the incubator since its gauges didn't look reliable. There was now a real reason to be responsible so all my students stepped up to the plate, and they were wonderful.

Doing this project year after year, the students' routines were well rehearsed, which encouraged the senior students to train the new students on what needed to be done to help the hatching process. I found that my biggest problem was to keep my students and their friends away from the equipment and control their involvement. This was a problem I was happy to have!

My students may have dealt with the eggs during the school hours, but they didn't feel the real inconvenience of incubating the eggs. All the books we read said that the eggs should be turned four to five times a day. The students would turn the eggs three times during school and then I would turn them once more before I left work which was usually around five or six o'clock in the evening. Unfortunately, that left one more turn for me to do at night. Maybe it wasn't critical to turn the eggs the fifth time, but I felt it was necessary to check the temperature. I only lived a half mile from the school so the drive was easy. The hard part was getting into my trailer at night.

My trailer, though by the playground, was also positioned at the back of the school right next to a wooded park. That meant I had to walk from my car through the poorly lit parking lot, along the side of the trailer, toward the back of the school to my front door. Who knows who or what could have been lurking underneath the trailer those many dark nights I went to check on the incubator? In retrospect, it was certainly a foolish thing to have done, but I couldn't bear the thought of a bird dying or not hatching because I had let the temperature get too high or too low. I just didn't trust the gauges on the incubator, and I wasn't about to disappoint the children.

I knew going at nine or ten o'clock at night was not very smart since the wooded park was known to have questionable people roaming in it at night. Understanding what could be looming in the dark, my heart would race so hard and so fast until I was safely back in my car. I finally got tired of being so frightened and decided to actually drive up to the entrance of my room. It was such a simple solution, but it would never have been approved, especially by the first principal. From the parking lot, I would slowly drive up over the curb, then over the grass and along the sidewalk. I would park my car by the trailer, shining my lights underneath the trailer, which also lit up the entranceway to my room. My naive thinking allowed me to believe I was safe by doing this. Thankfully, regardless of my stupidity, nothing bad ever happened. Well, at least nothing bad happened to me.

My first full year teaching and the first year we incubated eggs, a few of my night visits were spent driving in the pouring rain. One time during a long soaking rain, when I drove up onto the grass and the soil was so saturated, I made several muddy ruts a few feet long. At the time, I didn't pay too much attention to the ruts but the next morning I walked by the office and overheard a couple of teachers and the principal talking. The principal was swearing about the thoughtless high school students who had been driving on school property. When I heard his angry unsubstantiated accusations of high school kids, I invited myself into the group. I asked him how he knew the damage on the school grounds was caused by high school kids. He looked at me as if I was just an annoyance deflating his energies toward the issue at hand. Quickly, as if swatting a fly, he snapped, "Who else would do something so stupid?" First, I thought to myself, kids weren't the only people to do stupid things and secondly, at 10:30 on a foggy and rainy night with eerie shadows dancing around, it wasn't so stupid. I know I should have told him that I had caused the damage, but he already didn't like me, and I couldn't find the courage to give him any more ammunition, so I walked to my room holding on to my secret.

Checking the eggs during the work-week wasn't the only inconvenience because over the weekends, the eggs still had to be turned. Fortunately, there were always two other teachers hatching birds in their classrooms during the same time period, so over the weekends, we would take turns turning everyone's eggs. Unfortunately for me, during spring break, the other two teachers would confidently take their eggs and their new incubators to their homes. I couldn't bring myself to move our archaic incubator for many reasons. What I told everyone was that I didn't want to move it to my place since the incubator was so old, rickety, and seemingly unreliable. The truth was that I was afraid that I would drop the incubator and the eggs! That meant that over my spring breaks, I would go to school four to five times a day. I may have grumbled silently knowing that what I was doing was absurd, but I also knew I wouldn't have done it any other way.

In our classroom, we kept a calendar showing how many days were left until *The Day!* As the days were crossed off, the excitement grew. My students would bring their friends to class before and after school and sometimes even come to class when they weren't scheduled, which didn't bother me, as long as they didn't get in trouble with their classroom teacher. I was always happy for my students to visit during this project and show off to their friends. Usually, the students would come in quietly, sit down and just stare, so they were never a distraction or a bother. Even my students who were labeled hyperactive would glue themselves by the incubator with fixed eyes, waiting—waiting for the first egg to move. When all the false alarms were over, and the eggs really started moving, joyful hysteria erupted! Over those five years, I never was able to control that moment with the students. I guess it was mainly because I was right there in the middle of the commotion enjoying the special occasion as much as my students.

After everyone calmed down, still and silent bodies resumed their positions with wide eyes waiting for the next event; the first crack. The students would become much more serious and anxious at this time because seeing the eggs move around and hearing the birds chirp inside the shells truly bothered them. Because of their concern, they created some hard and fast rules: the trailer door was never allowed to be slammed, people could only whisper and everyone had to be light-footed around the classroom so not to disturb our treasures. Though I knew these restrictions were not necessary, it was fun to watch them police each other. On the rare occasion a classmate would forget the rules, he or she quickly received stern reprimands from the others. I never had to say anything; I just followed the rules.

There was always great anticipation to see the *first* bird appear. Unfortunately, no one ever got to see that happen because every year, the first bird would already have ventured out of its shell either through the night or early morning, while no one was watching. Our new addition may have already hatched but I loved being able to watch our miracle during the calm of the morning. Though I loved watching my students gaze at the birds, I selfishly enjoyed my early mornings when I could quietly contemplate these wonders all by myself.

When my students would see the newly hatched birds, their faces would range from ear to ear smiles of total joy to deeply creviced frowns of genuine concern for the birds in their struggle. It was almost impossible to not feel something as we watched the eggs and birds knock and bounce each other around. With every successful bird hatching, there came a little sigh of relief from each of us.

Every year, there were always a few eggs that didn't hatch. After waiting a week past the due date, making sure the birds weren't just late bloomers or that we miscalculated their hatch date, we would go outside and open the eggs to see what stage the bird stopped growing. Every year, I described the possible sights and smells they could encounter. Through very good acting on my part, showing only investigative interest and not my true fear that a bird might still be alive, I only had to personally open one egg over the five years since there were always students eager to volunteer to help.

While scrutinizing the unhatched bird, there were the usual muttered comments such as "Gross!" or "I'm going to throw-up!" or "It stinks!" That is until they realized that I wasn't reacting or participating. I tried to squelch any inappropriate comments immediately. Sadly, though I worked very hard to avoid confrontations with students, there were always a few who wouldn't be quiet. They were probably just emulating how someone they knew had reacted to an uncomfortable situation, but I had no tolerance for irritating and distracting behavior. I also didn't want them to taint how my other students viewed the experience with the eggs being opened. The few students who didn't quiet down after my warning were always sent back to our room. The students had learned that if they blew their warning, there was no more discussion on my part, and it was fruitless to argue, so they would go to the room with just a few face-saving grumbles.

I did learn, however, never to deny the experiences to the students who were turned away. I realized that the reprimanded children would usually continue their bad behavior long after their punishment was over, probably trying to save their dignity and cover up their frustration from being left out. In the case of hatching eggs, I would save an egg or the remains, for the punished student to open or see at a later time. At that time, I could show the student how to act without peer influence and expose him or her to what the other students experienced.

I was exceptionally fortunate for the first four years that when our birds hatched, they lived. With the other two classes that hatched eggs, they would have birds hatch but then die, so we would talk about *their* birds dying. That was easy; they weren't our birds. I didn't realize how lucky I was, being sheltered from that gruesome ordeal of dealing with dead birds; that is, until my fifth spring.

On our fifth spring of incubating eggs, we tried something new. Instead of chickens or quail, we chose ducks. That same year we were also given a brand-new state of the art incubator. We thought we were so lucky to get eleven fertile duck eggs as well as a new incubator. Though ducks took longer to hatch, we all thought we were on Easy Street with our new incubator. Well, that was at least what I thought until our ducks were hatching days before they were due and then dying. It was emotionally painful for me because I had to maintain my teacher's appearance when all I really wanted to do was cry as I watched our ducks die not knowing what had gone wrong.

Our neighborhood veterinarian had gotten used to my family and me calling him for the strangest of animal problems. This time was no exception. After describing my plight with the ducks, he explained that sometime near the end of the ducks' incubation, the temperature must have gone higher, speeding up the ducks' development. That meant that the ducks were hatching before they were actually strong enough to survive. Using our old thermometer, we checked the temperature of the incubator only to find out that our new, good-for-nothing, modernized incubator had a faulty temperature gauge.

In a last-ditch effort to save our three remaining eggs, we quickly improvised a new incubating procedure. Every thirty minutes a student was to check the temperature. If it was too hot, the student would tilt the lid and blow into the incubator, cooling the eggs. We never had to worry about the incubator getting too cool, that was for sure. On my last visit at night, not to check the eggs but instead to check the temperature, I managed to get a constant temperature by leaving the lid slightly cracked open. These three ducks just had to live. It was tearing me up inside watching the others die, knowing I couldn't stop it.

With the ducks that had died, I had a new problem: what to do with them? Should I put them in the dumpster or should I bury them? What was sanitary, moral, or right? To some people, this might not have been a problem. For me, it was a real dilemma. I decided to admit to my students how confused and awkward I felt dealing with this situation. I guess my openness got them talking about all the possible options. After lengthy discussions, none of us chose the dumpster. Our decision was to bury our ducks in the woods behind the school and give them individual funerals.

With the three ducks left, I wasn't sure how I would

handle the situation if none of them lived. The gloomy atmosphere in the room, the somber faces and the moping children were more than I could bear. No cheering kids getting underfoot, no friends trickling in to sneak a peek at our ducks. It was horrible! That was until one of the three eggs started cracking!

Hope sprang into our hearts, smiles danced back on our faces, eyes sparkled, and friends came. Unfortunately, this joyful time didn't last. After the duck made a hole just large enough for us to see his beak, he stopped hatching. For almost one hour that morning, we watched his beak move slower and slower. He seemed so weak, and I knew we were watching this bird slowly die. I couldn't just stand around and watch this duck die, so I ran back to the office to call the veterinarian again, leaving my students in Mrs. Martin's care. I had to see if there was something we could do to save this precious creature.

The very patient veterinarian explained again that our duck wasn't ready to come out but still cracked the egg. With the hole in the shell and not enough strength to get out quickly, he was drying out and was probably stuck to the shell. He told me to increase the humidity in the incubator and explained that I would need to lubricate the duck so it could break free from the shell. This kind and gentle man then offered me two options to help moisten the duck. One was to buy a solution at the drug store, which would work quite well. It may have been the best option, but I knew that choice wasn't possible since I couldn't leave school to make the purchase and if I waited for school to be over, the duck would probably be dead.

With an anxious tone, I inquired what my other option was. Though it was quite simple, I couldn't help but laugh when I heard what my other option was because he told me I was going to use my spit! The veterinarian explained that I would need to spit through the hole on a regular basis in order to help free the duck from its shell. Although I was laughing, I could tell that he was serious, so that is exactly what I did.

There is no easy or tactful way to explain to a room full of students that the best way we could help our duck was to spit on him! Needless to say, the rest of our day was hilarious. Every fifteen to twenty minutes, whatever we were doing was constantly being disrupted by a student reminding me it was time to spit. In order to do this, I would open the incubator lid, bend over and prepare to spit into the small hole right onto our little duck. I couldn't believe what I was doing. Where was this written in textbooks I had studied? Where was this in my job description?

As I was ready to spit one time, I looked up and saw eleven wide-eyed children intently watching me prepare to spit onto the duck. In my mind, I quickly ran a scenario of what answer these children would give to their parents that evening when they were asked what happened at school? I know students sometimes don't clearly explain things (not that this could ever be explained), but I could hear their answer, "Watched Miss Chandler spit!" Somewhere in their explanation of the day, the reason for this situation could easily be lost. I couldn't dwell on that thought for long though, because we had a duck to save.

After a series of spitting sessions, I stopped feeling stupid because our duck was moving more and more and the hole gradually grew larger. It may have been guarded, but our excitement rose again. Then it happened. He finally broke free! Screams, tears, and hugs were shared as we stood in awe watching our miracle baby duck wobbling around the incubator! The joy we experienced that day was fabulous.

As usual, the children got to choose the name for the bird. With all the drama wrapped around our duck-hatching project, the classroom teachers generously agreed to allow all my students to gather in my room right after our duck had hatched. We may have looked and felt like sardines packed inside my room, but I needed (and wanted) everyone present to name our precious miracle. In the past, this was a long and difficult task trying to get everyone to agree on a name. This time though, we all quickly agreed. Who could argue? There was no better name to represent our duck and his struggle than the name Spit Bucket! And so the little duck was named.

The other two ducks hatched the next day with no problems. Over the following ten days, before we gave them to a friend who had ducks and chickens as yard pets, we watched our three ducks grow. The last two that hatched were much stronger and larger but neither was as special or as close to our hearts as our little runt Spit Bucket!

Punished for Doing Well

OVER A PERIOD of three months, Colton's parents, his classroom teacher, and I were all very excited to see that he was consistently doing well in the fourth grade. Over this three-month period, Colton's time attending my class had been cut back gradually so he could spend more and more time in his regular classroom. Checking all the markers for improvement and taking what we thought was *everything* into consideration, all the people involved with Colton agreed to have his I.E.P. rewritten to put him on a consultation basis with me. This would allow him to stay full-time in his regular classroom, and I would basically work with his teacher to assist in any areas of concern she might have. We were all so proud of Colton and thrilled with his wonderful accomplishments. What a success story! Or was it?

The first three weeks with Colton not coming to my room went so smoothly that Miss Spencer, his classroom teacher, felt she didn't even need my help. By the end of the fifth week, the situation with Colton took a drastic turn. Miss Spencer came to my room after school to share some mounting concerns about Colton. In a nutshell, she explained that he simply stopped doing his work well and basically just sat in class. He didn't get involved, didn't ask questions, and avoided any type of contact with her. Miss Spencer described what she had done to motivate him but nothing seemed to work so she asked me for any other ideas that might help her get Colton back on track. As I asked questions to understand more of what was going on, I devised some approaches that might help. Disappointingly, over the next two weeks, Colton just kept falling behind.

Miss Spencer and I had a conference with his parents, hoping they could shed some light on the problem but sadly, they were hoping for the same from us. At different times, we all had asked him if the work was too hard or even too easy but he always gave that simple answer, "It's fine," but unfortunately, Colton's work and attitude just kept saying the contrary.

One afternoon, I had a free block of time and was walking back to my room. I saw Colton was on the playground, so I asked Miss Spencer if I could talk with him in my room for a short while. She happily approved so I called for Colton, and he came running immediately. As he ran up to me, he responded, "Yes, Miss Chandler?" I asked him if he would come with me to my room for a while and he replied with an energetic "Sure!" Then he proceeded to run to the door of my trailer.

I asked Colton to sit down with me so we could talk. Though he sat right down, something in my voice must not have been normal because he looked up at me with such a hurt look, and he quietly asked if he was in trouble. Trying to calm his nerves, I said he wasn't in trouble at all, but I did want to see how he was doing in Miss Spencer's class. He said, "Fine." I asked how the work was. Again, he said, "Fine." I asked how the other students in his class were. He said, "Fine." I continued with how were his parents? How was his brother? How was he feeling?" All his answers were an uninformative "fine."

Not getting anywhere with the subtle approach, I confessed to Colton that I knew his grades were plummeting and that he wasn't participating in his class anymore. I admitted that I was confused hearing this since I was certain he could do the work. He acknowledged the work was fine, but he revealed he hadn't realized that if he did well in Miss Spencer's class, he would have to stop coming to my room. All he wanted now was to come back to my room, and he thought that would happen if he couldn't do the work.

Talk about coming out of left field. I never would have guessed that reason. I sat directly in front of him, trying not to look like I was melting inside, and I asked him to explain why he wanted to come back to my room. I was astonished with all the reasons he had floating around in that precious head of his. First, Colton told me that though there was a great deal of work to do in my room, it was fun and never seemed boring. Then, he got emotional telling me how much he really liked and missed the other kids in my class and that he enjoyed helping them. He continued opening up by admitting he didn't want to miss all the projects that we did in the classroom, like hatching eggs every year.

Colton explained that in his regular classroom he just did worksheets, workbooks, and read boring stories. He sighed, saying that during math class, which was his favorite subject, the teacher would introduce a new skill, and he and the other students would be given a worksheet to do at his or her desk and then given another worksheet to do for homework. Colton continued by describing his reading group as being too crowded. Because of the number of students in his group, he rarely got called on to answer a question, so he just stopped raising his hand. All his explanations were hard to hear but the last one stung the most since it brought back such painful memories of my own. He whispered (as if he thought he would get in trouble) that he didn't feel important in the other class but in mine, he felt very important!

Colton rarely showed any emotions and this occasion was no exception. I, on the other hand, was very emotional and showed it. This was no exception for me either as I began tearing up. I tried to clarify that he was very important to Miss Spencer and explained that things were just different between the two classes. I also assured him that he would always be important to me in or out of my class. I apologized for not understanding his take on the situation and for not knowing how he felt in regard to his new placement. No one had ever talked with him. We just assumed he would be as excited as we were.

I promised Colton that I would talk with Miss Spencer, but explained from that point on, if he really wanted to be back in my class, he had to bring his grades up and prove he deserved to be there. Hugging him, I qualified my statement by saying that only students who tried hard and did their best got to be in my room. He looked at me with his big brown eyes, almost showing a smile, and enthusiastically replied, "Yes, ma'am!"

Miss Spencer totally agreed with the change, and we started the new program back in my room as soon as his parents gave their permission. It was absolutely wonderful having Colton back in my classroom! I hadn't realized how much I missed him and how much he added to our class's atmosphere. Though Colton only came to my room for forty-five minutes a day, which was during independent time in his regular classroom, it seemed to be enough to satisfy him and keep the upward trend with his work during the rest of the school year.

If parents and educators would listen to what Colton said about his classroom situations, they might learn what is really needed to successfully reach students so we can teach them. What children want and desperately need is human one-to-one contact. They need personal encouragement for what they are working through. They need laughter and friendship. They need someone to listen to them, play with them, and cry with them. They also need someone to guide and discipline them. Not surprisingly ... none of these cost money!

I taught in a rickety trailer with extremely inadequate supplies and yet the progress made with each child in that room was amazing! What I did didn't cost money. It wasn't that I was an outstanding teacher either. I gave my students time and committed attention to what each one of them needed. Many of the successes my students achieved were when I was least trained or experienced. Giving my students time and individual attention made them see and feel that they were important and that they mattered.

Unfortunately, most families and schools are getting farther from the personal approach, so our children lose out. More money won't help what ails schools (and families for that matter) in all situations. Giving time and personal attention will. Maybe, just maybe, a ten and a half year old knows more than the adults do about what is important in schools and even in our homes!

Moving On

AFTER FIVE AND a half emotional, painful, yet glorious years, I decided to leave teaching (for a while). Initially, I left because I knew I needed to make more money since the pittance I made barely covered my expenses. Over time, I realized that though I did need to make more money, it was also time for me move on. I had learned so many wonderful lessons and hopefully taught many too, but it was time for new adventures. Unknown to me at that juncture in my life, what I had learned and experienced inside that rickety, old trailer was just preparing me for the new adventures ahead that were going to be just as emotional, painful, and absolutely glorious!

Thanks and Gratitude to Many

THERE ARE SO many people I want to thank for their influence in my life and for the stories in this book.

First of all, I want to thank Dr. Coble. He is the person who suggested this project in the first place years ago. After hearing many of my tales, he encouraged me to write down my stories. His teaching techniques and sage advice are still positively affecting my life decades after attending his class.

Many thanks to Lee Heinrich and Kevin Snyder, along with their team members from Write Way Publishing Company. They patiently taught and guided me through the many decisions that needed to be made in order to actually "publish" this book.

My absolute gratitude pours out to the children I have taught found within these pages and the many not mentioned. They are all such important people and outstanding influences in my life.

I want to thank my parents, Ferris and Mary Jane Chandler for the upbringing they offered me as well as the love and support I received while I lived through these and many other challenges. They are without a doubt exceptional parents.

I am so grateful for my sister, Cindy Chappell. She always had a listening ear and the patience of a saint as I would ramble on and on about all that I was dealing with throughout my journey. She is an incredibly wonderful person and heaven-sent friend.

As a teacher, I appreciate the fabulous professionals I had the honor to work with and for. They helped me make my way through the ins and outs of the education world.

Oddly, I also am grateful to the not-so-fabulous and maybe even the few downright horrible people I had to work with and for because sometimes these were the people who really challenged me to be the person I wanted to become.

I am indebted to my husband, Chris, for his undying support to this seemingly endless project. He never gave up on the project or me. For that and many, many other reasons, I love him dearly!

Then there are my children: Clarkson and Kylene. It is hard to accurately and adequately describe my love, admiration, and gratitude for and to them. My life has been so blessed because they are in my world. Because of them, I was fueled to finish this project and to have at least two copies—one for each of them—so they could learn what their mom's life was like when she was younger.

Most importantly, I want to thank God. There wouldn't be any wonderful stories to share about these exceptional students of mine had I not been in the absolute guidance of God. I didn't know it then, but looking back now, none of what transpired in this book would have happened without His nudges! He blessed me with a quirky personality that seemed to fit with what needed to be accomplished. I am awestruck by the masterful ways that He worked in my life, even when I wasn't aware of it. I am forever grateful to Him for trusting and entrusting me with the lives of so many precious children and for teaching me the greatest lesson of all: with love and commitment, *just do what works!*

About the Author

KATHERINE IS AN author and educational speaker. Whether in print or with the spoken word, Katherine guides her audiences to think for themselves so they can achieve the most successful and enriched lives they were meant to live. She does this by skillfully grabbing her audience's attention with her personal stories. Some stories in this book will make you laugh, some will make you cry, but they all will make you think!

Katherine has taught in the public and private sectors and homeschooled her own children for eleven and half years. She was also a director of a learning center in North Carolina and two centers in Hawai'i. Katherine now lives with her husband, nestled away in North Carolina.